BORDER CROSSINGS

BORDER CROSSINGS

Cross-Cultural Hermeneutics

Edited by D. N. Premnath

ORBIS BOOKS

Maryknoll, New York 10545

Copyright © 2007 by Devadasan N. Premnath.

Published by Orbis Books, Maryknoll, New York 10545-0308.

Manufactured in the United States of America.

Queries regarding rights and permissions should be addressed to:
Orbis Books, P.O. Box 308, Maryknoll, New York 10545-0308.

Library of Congress Cataloging-in-Publication Data

Border crossings : cross-cultural hermeneutics / edited by D.N. Premnath.
    p. cm.
    Includes bibliographical references.
    ISBN-13: 978-1-57075-745-7
    1. Bible – Criticism, interpretation, etc. 2. Bible – Hermeneutics.
3. Hermeneutics – Religious aspects – Christianity.   I. Premnath, D. N.
BS511.3.B66 2007
221.6 – dc22

                      2007023992

Essays in Honor of

R. S. Sugirtharajah

*Scholar, Thinker, and Friend,
for His Significant Contribution
to Postcolonial Biblical Criticism
and Cross-Cultural Hermeneutics*

CONTENTS

Part Three
PEDAGOGICAL PERSPECTIVES

Part Four
PERSONAL PERSPECTIVES

Foreword

A WORD OF GRATITUDE AND CONGRATULATIONS "FROM THE MARGIN"

Fernando F. Segovia

This volume of congratulations in honor of Professor Rasiah S. Sugirtharajah is well appointed and well deserved. The world of the academy is right in bestowing upon him its highest formal accolade, for he has done much indeed for the world of biblical studies. Indeed, when the history of biblical criticism over the crucial years encompassing the turn of the century — from the last decade of the twentieth into the first decade of the twenty-first — is written, his name and his work will feature prominently in its development and its direction. To be sure, such a history will be one undertaken "from the margin," to invoke a distinctive signifier of his writing and his thinking, not from the mainstream. It shall be a proper recognition by the margin of one of its own — a recognition that the present volume wisely and prophetically marks in advance.

The figure and the message of Sugi, as he is affectionately and respectfully known among his many friends and colleagues, first appeared on the global biblical scene with the publication in 1991 of his edited volume *Voices from the Margin: Interpreting the Bible in the Third World* (Orbis Books). At this time, he held the position of Lecturer in Third World Theologies at Selly Oak Colleges in Birmingham, England, after a period of teaching in India at Serampore College in Calcutta and Tamilnadu Theological Seminary in Madurai. This volume was a key contribution in the area of contextual hermeneutics, the first of several such major compilations since then. Given its subsequent editions in 1995 and 2006, the volume also serves, by way of its changing introductions and postscripts, as an ideal way to track and demarcate the rich and complex path of his constantly expanding critical vision as well as his rapidly multiplying scholarly activities. This is especially true of the third edition of 2006, which marks the fifteenth anniversary of both the publication of the collection and of his presence on the international scene. Here we find the telling addition of a new section of entries, "Postcolonial Readings," reflecting a most important turn in his life from contextual hermeneutics to postcolonial interpretation, which takes place around the time of the second edition of 1995. At this point, he holds the rank of Professor of Biblical Studies at the University of Birmingham, England, his doctoral alma mater.

I should like to summarize his decisive role in the discipline and the profession over the course of these fifteen years of work. At the time of his debut in 1991, biblical criticism had already witnessed a series of important developments: first, the emergence of literary criticism and sociocultural criticism beginning around 1975, in a breakaway from the long-dominant historical-critical model of interpretation; second, an increasing emphasis on the process of reading and reader-constructs within literary criticism and on social and cultural models of contextualization in sociocultural criticism, steadily through the 1980s; third, a growing attention to the question of power relationships in both texts and interpretations and thus the rise of ideological criticism, beginning with feminist criticism and materialist criticism in the 1970s and followed by minority criticism in the 1980s. The move throughout, inexorable in retrospect, is toward ever greater focus on the real readers of the texts, of all sorts, and on the contextual and perspectival nature of all interpretation. It is this move that Professor Sugirtharajah captured and embodied in eminent fashion in the first edition of *Voices from the Margin* of 1991. Fifteen years later, biblical criticism has experienced the full eruption of ideological criticism: first, through greater sophistication in the conceptualization and application of feminist, materialist, and minority criticism; second, through the addition of postcolonial criticism and queer criticism; and finally, through beginning calls for intersectional criticism. The move throughout, seemingly inexorable as well, has been toward an ever greater sense of complexity in the analysis of power relationships in both texts and criticism. It is this move that Professor

Sugirtharajah records and signifies so well in the third edition of *Voices from the Margin* of 2006.

From 1991 to 2006, therefore, an initial, driving interest in contextual criticism, ultimately inspired by the hermeneutics of liberation and focused on faces and voices outside the mainstream, gave way to — or, perhaps better put, transformed itself into — a sustained, compelling pursuit of postcolonial criticism, now grounded in postcolonial studies across the academic spectrum (with emphasis on cultural production more than on material matrix) yet still centered on voices and faces not of the mainstream. One could envision a move toward greater theorization in interpretation: from general attention and low-level problematization, toward pointed analysis and high-level problematization of issues of power, real readers, and contextual-perspectival interpretation.

All of this, I would add, alongside ever broader involvement in theological studies, not only with a pan-Asian focus but also with a worldwide non-Western concern and ever more numerous publication projects, both by way of personal contributions and collective endeavors. And, throughout, that ever present and ever recurring "from the margins": puncturing the mainstream; foregrounding the marginal; networking the peripheral; envisioning an alternative future; seeking justice and dignity. Truly, then, a remarkable academic — and, I would add, intensely human — achievement, well rewarded by this congratulatory volume, in rightful anticipation of a well-deserved leading place in the history of biblical criticism, as written "from the margins," for the margins and the center alike. For all this, Sugi, all of us, your colleagues and friends, stand in profound admiration and gratitude — and I, in particular, for the singular opportunity to have shared in so many forums, so many projects, and so many visions together over these years. Our best wishes, then, for the future: May your work continue for many years to come, and may we be granted the privilege of a thirtieth-anniversary edition of *Voices from the Margin* in 2022.

INTRODUCTION

D. N. PREMNATH

Two factors were instrumental in the birth of this collection. The first critical factor was the desire to provide a forum for addressing the phenomenon of diasporic interpretation. Today many biblical and theological scholars who have had their upbringing and education in one sociocultural context find themselves working in a totally different cultural context for a variety of reasons. The focus is not on the reasons for their displacement but rather on the experience of negotiating multiple worlds and boundaries and what this means for their work. The second motivating factor for this volume is to honor the work of R. S. Sugirtharajah, who has done significant pioneering work in the area of postcolonial criticism in relation to biblical studies. Among other things, Sugirtharajah has consistently sought to address the diasporic interpretation in his works. It is fitting, therefore, that this volume is presented in honor of Sugirtharajah's contributions to a greater understanding of cross-cultural hermeneutics.

The meaning of the term "border crossing" can range from a literal sense to a more metaphorical one. In this age of transnationalism and globalization the term has taken on a wider connotation. Crossing borders has not only become a necessity but also is indispensable in some sense. We can begin to understand the usefulness of the border-crossing construct in a variety of ways, including those that are national, racial, social, and cultural, to name a few. Borders or boundaries are primarily markers that divide one entity from another. Some key questions arise: Who determines borders? What is the nature of borders? What are the benefits or consequences of having borders?

Those who cross borders recognize the power of the borders to include or exclude. Although there is an aura of fixedness surrounding borders, the opposite may be true. Borders designate at once not only the line

1

where something ends but also where something new begins.[1] Homi Bhabha points out that borders or boundaries give rise to in-between spaces that serve as alternative sites for generating meaning.[2] The in-between spaces are intriguing for that very reason. Being in between borders gives one the ability to recognize where the borders are and the identity they delineate.[3] It also provides a vantage point from which to examine and critique. The act of border crossing opens up new locations for conversation and new alliances.

Sugirtharajah's works on postcolonial criticism have important implications for discussions on border crossing. The postcolonial discourse that Sugirtharajah expounds in his works and describes at the end of this collection relates to border crossing in three distinct ways. First, postcolonial discourse challenges the legacy of colonialism by exposing assumptions and characterizations that benefit the dominant majority and restrict and deprive the Other. Postcolonial discourse creates a "place" for the Other to speak.[4] Second, postcolonial discourse redefines the relationship between the margins and the mainstream. The relationship is not in terms of polarities between the West and the rest. In fact, postcolonial discourse warns against simplistic representations by idealizing one and demonizing the other. Each entity shares histories of "being complicit, resistant, victim and accomplice."[5] Third, postcolonial discourse challenges any homogeneous and static representation of identity for the colonized. The purpose is to nuance and de-center but not to dismiss. The colonized need a space in which to speak so that inherited histories and practices can be challenged and transformed. In this sense, postcolonial discourse facilitates the act of border crossing as it opens up new possibilities for liberating speech and practice.[6]

The Role of Social Identity

Central to the discussion of cross-cultural hermeneutics is the question of an individual's social identity. The matter of social identity, however, is complex. The prominent tendency among us is to see things in either-or categories, but social identity is multifaceted. Race or ethnicity, perhaps more visible than others, is only one of many facets. Through our lived experience and the various positions we occupy in society, we create a complex sociocultural identity. This complex identity is due to the various cultural markers and meaning systems that constitute our total makeup.[7] For instance, an Asian American may be a member of a Protestant denomination, belong to the middle class, and be part of an entrepreneurial class. Or an African American may be a Catholic, a member of the upper middle-class, and may belong to a managerial class. Each of these cultural markers carries with it a distinct set of meaning and value systems, sometimes complementary and other times quite contradictory. These markers contribute to a complex sociocultural identity. Further, the same cultural markers may very well set apart members belonging to the same social group because members of a particular social group may not necessarily define themselves in exactly the same way. Some may see their ethnic identity as central and others as background. But surrounded by a dominant majority, whether the minority groups see their identity as central or not, the fact remains that placed in an unequal society, members of a minority group have one thing in common. They share a burden of social — and economic and political — challenges in an unequal society.

In reflecting on identity, one also has to be mindful of designations or labels, which tend to lump individuals from different backgrounds into one. A classic case in point is the term "Asian." This term may be used to refer to a Chinese-speaking Christian living in Hong Kong as well as a Tamil-speaking Brahmin living in Chennai, India, and many other combinations in between. The same thing is true of a designation such as "Hispanic" or "Latino/Latina." The pertinent factor here is that the dominant group tends to lump individuals in a group and attribute certain stereotypes to that group. These characterizations are usually rooted in assumptions that may be implicit or unacknowledged, and yet presumed upon according to the dominant group's norm.

These assumptions often manifest themselves in cultural practices and language. Forms of oppression manifest themselves not only through covert, conscious prejudice and discrimination but also through unconscious attitudes and behaviors predicated upon the dominant group's cultural norm. Often times these assumptions are implicit in the language that is used and the cultural practices that are prevalent. People belonging to marginal groups can never fully escape being perceived as belonging to a particular social group.[8] For example, an ethnic woman who excels in her work may be seen as exceptional or not representative of her group. If the ethnic woman does poorly, however, she may be seen as exhibiting the limitations of the group to which she belongs.

Whether she does well or poorly, she is not judged on the basis of her individual capability but rather as a member of a social group. Contrast this with an instance involving a member of the dominant group. For instance, a white male is rarely judged by his maleness or whiteness. If he does well in his job, he is acknowledged as a qualified individual. If he does poorly, he is not judged in reference to his group but only as an inadequate employee. The blame is attributed to him alone.

Social Identity and Pedagogy

Since many of the diasporic interpreters are engaged in the teaching profession, their social identity has serious implications for pedagogy. "Pedagogy" is often used synonymously with teaching or a teaching style. Most definitions relate pedagogy to teaching as an agency, a profession, or a practice. As a concept, however, pedagogy draws attention to a broader reality. A closer look at pedagogy reveals a process involving three aspects or entities: (1) the one who teaches, (2) the one who learns, and (3) the learning that transpires in the interaction between the teacher and the learner.[9] Even though how and what one teaches is of critical importance, it cannot be divested from how and what one actually learns. In other words, pedagogy is not just about teaching, but it is also about the interaction or exchange involving the teacher, the learner, and the knowledge they together produce.

As teachers, who we are as individuals affects both how and what we teach. It also affects how we view our students. Our cultural identities do inform and influence our professional identity, and the cultural assumptions we carry around affect how we see others, especially our students. At the same time, as teachers we need to be cognizant that the same is true of our students as well. Who they are as individuals, with their cultural assumptions, affects what and how they learn. It also affects how they view the teacher. Cultural awareness on the part of both parties is critical.

Teaching, learning, and cultural awareness are inseparable. If pedagogical practices are devoid of cultural awareness and sensitivity, a gulf is bound to exist between those teaching and those learning. Teaching is communicating. Adequate communication can happen in and through the meaning systems and worldviews that teachers and learners bring to the table. The process of pedagogy aims at relating the culture, the curriculum, and the process of learning.

This relationship between culture and pedagogy raises some key issues. From a cultural perspective, teachers and learners enter the world of the classroom with certain assumptions and expectations. Culture has to do with values and meaning systems that people create and use consciously or unconsciously in their everyday lives and activities.[10] Learners as well as teachers bring their values and meaning systems into the classroom. At a deeper level, pedagogy does help in facilitating meaning systems. As teachers who we are as individuals and the values and meaning systems we bring impact how we teach and what we teach. The same is true of our students. If we concede the importance of this link, we realize the challenge in the pedagogical endeavor. Some tough questions surface: What is the role of the teacher in the meaning-facilitation process? Given the power relations within a classroom, who has the upper hand in facilitating values or meaning systems? Is there such a thing as common culture?[11] These are explosive questions. They are intellectually challenging and emotionally charged, and our professional training does not always prepare us to address emotionally and socially charged issues in the classroom.

Raising emotionally charged issues such as colonialism, oppression, racism, and sexism, among others, is hardly a neutral activity. I suspect that in most classrooms our particular social and cultural identities tend to remain in the background. But when dealing with issues of oppression, social identity becomes crucial. Who we are as individuals is often central to the way in which we understand and respond to issues of oppression. Whether we are part of the privileged group or the minority group invariably influences our response and perspective.

Border Pedagogy

At this point, I would like to introduce the idea of "border pedagogy" in relation to "border crossing." The concept of border pedagogy initially came on the educational philosophy scene in the 1980s. It is expounded more fully and in a challenging manner in the works of Henry Giroux, upon whose insights I once again draw. The emergence of border pedagogy is a reaction against and an alternative to the traditional approach to education as a "banking system." The objection is not only in reference to the mode of transferring knowledge but also the principle it values.

The traditional approach sees education as a transferal of content from the all-knowing sage to the empty vessels that occupy the seats of learning. The principle it values is that the teacher is there to impart "correct" ways to learn and understand the world. This system or approach benefits and rewards those who are willing to play along with the system. The beneficiaries for the most part are members of the dominant majority. Border pedagogy is critical of this banking system because it functions to exclude those who are not part of the privileged. In an effort to offer a corrective, border pedagogy puts forward an alternative in its open and inclusive approach to teaching and learning; it values the cultural diversity, varied histories, and different understandings present in the classroom.[12]

The term "border" sharply captures the dominant tendency to establish borders or boundaries based on the either-or binaries within Western thought, for example those of self/other, white/black, male/female, West/rest, and culture/nature.[13] The dominant group defines, structures, and thereby dominates all constituted as Other. Border pedagogy provides a pedagogical alternative for learners to identify and be critical of these borders that are used to set apart entities and peoples. On the positive side, border pedagogy encourages learners to find "the spaces between the borders."[14] This is helpful because the reality of people's lives is too complex to fit into neat categories. People cross and re-cross boundaries as a matter of course. Border pedagogy operates on that assumption and in fact seeks "to create spaces for these experiences to be expressed, valued, and thought through by students and teachers alike."[15]

The basic premise of border pedagogy is that the process of learning entails crossing borders. These are not only physical borders but also cultural borders that have been historically constructed and socially organized.[16] Border pedagogy enables learners to identify and engage these borders. By negotiating these multiple borders, learners, in effect, are generating multiple references of meaning, knowledge, social relations, and values.[17] Existing assumptions underlying dominant definitions of reality get challenged and critically read. It is not enough "to read these codes critically but also to learn the limits of such codes, including the ones they use to construct their own narratives and histories."[18] In the act of border crossing, existing social relations, power equations, cultural codes, and identities become subject to challenges and shifts. As Giroux points out, "the terrain of learning becomes inextricably linked to the shifting parameters of place, identity, history and power."[19]

The use of border pedagogy has some important implications. One of the critical results of using border pedagogy is its ability to expose the dominant definitions of reality. It enables the learner to recognize cultural codes and social practices that marginalize or even repress alternative ways of perceiving. It exposes how representations and practices that marginalize the Other are actively coded and imparted. Particularly damaging are the tendencies to see and represent the Other as deficient according to the standards set by the dominant group. Such representations can be challenged effectively by offering new categories and strategies for learning. The models of the dominant culture need no longer be the sole basis for defining what constitutes proper knowledge. Instead, forms of knowledge originating from the margins can become tools to redefine the complex experiences of learners that fall outside the framework of a "single, unitary culture."[20] As learners cross borders, alternative forms of knowledge emerge and the dominant definitions of reality come under closer scrutiny. Border pedagogy results in reshaping and reconfiguring boundaries. In Giroux's words, "border pedagogy decenters as it remaps."[21]

Border pedagogy also highlights an important aspect of social identity. It provides a conceptual framework with which to address the complex identity of an individual. Individuals embody multiple cultural markers that punctuate their identity. And, as Giroux points out, "there is no single pre-determined relationship between a cultural code and the subject position a student occupies."[22] Even though one's class, race, and gender may influence one's response, border pedagogy recognizes that (1) it does not predetermine a single stereotypical response; (2) learners, teachers, and others "read and write culture at multiple levels";[23] and members belonging to the same social group may respond differently. In other words, one's position along the lines of racial, ethnic, class, and gender particularities does not predetermine how one leans toward a particular ideology, how one reads a particular text, or how one responds to particular forms of oppression.[24]

What do diversity and differences in perspective mean for pedagogy? How does one allow these divergent perspectives to be expressed in a classroom and yet be able to produce something positive? Here Giroux turns to Foucault's idea of counter-memory.[25] According to Foucault, counter-memory is a discourse of critique and transformation. It is a critique not only of the past but also the current codes. This critique helps us "to understand and change the present by placing it in a new relation to the past."[26] It is a critical reading not only of how the past informs the present but also of how the present informs the past. The ultimate purpose, however, is not just dismantling critique but also creating a constructive vision. Memory or remembrance functions in one of two ways. It can function as counter-memory, as indicated above, or, as Smith points out, as custom.[27] Custom is a discourse of continuity in which knowledge and practice are seen as deposits to be transmitted and inherited. Hence the discourse of custom often resorts to the familiar refrain of "This is the way it has always been done."

In this respect counter-memory and custom are opposite discourses. Counter-memory may be seen as subversive for its critical stance. But as a pedagogical concept, counter-memory educates both teachers and learners. It exposes how perceptions and representations concerning minority groups marginalize and devalue them. It points up the tensions, contradictions, and omissions between the representations of the minority groups by themselves and those by the dominant culture. It also alerts us that we may be complicit in aligning with the dominant perspectives and power relations. By creating such awareness, it enables us to transform such relations and perceptions.[28] This kind of recognition and awareness is essential for the minority groups to reclaim their histories, voices, and visions.[29] It is through such consciousness-raising that border pedagogy is able to create a new forum for alternative discourses. It is able to provide a safe haven for rewriting minority cultural narratives by enabling them to speak from their experiences and histories.

Border pedagogy not only enables learners to articulate their voices and memories but also educates them to critically engage their own histories and to critically examine the grounds on which their own representations have been built. It is important for teachers to facilitate the critical appropriation of horizons — that of the learners and their own. The function of effective pedagogy is to question and critically evaluate rather than simply celebrate one's differences. It is in and through such a critical engaging that experiences can be remade or, as Giroux calls it, "re-territorialized."[30] Re-territorializing refers to the process of not only being able to locate specific histories and identities but also being able to transform and make them anew.

From a pedagogical point of view, teachers have a crucial role to play. It is a tremendous challenge to exist and operate within social, cultural, and political borders that are multiple and complex. Rather than seeing this as a disadvantage, it may be beneficial to recognize that we are in a unique position of being able to deepen our own understanding of the diverse subjectivities of our learners. Border pedagogy can be effective only if teachers can facilitate a meaningful educational experience. This begins always by affirming the stories, voices, and experiences of the learners. But it is not enough to simply affirm; it is equally important for teachers to provide their students with a language and framework to critically examine their histories and voices. Part of this critical examination has to do with collectively engaging with others and their histories. This has implications for life beyond the classroom. Pedagogy does not begin and end in the classroom. What teachers and learners do in the classroom reflects and enacts the values of the wider society, and it has the potential to reinforce the status quo or bring forth transformation. In order for transformation to occur what is required is a pedagogy that can relate to the sociocultural position of "any learning group and the positions of the individuals within."[31]

Organization of the Book

One of the elements common to the present collection of essays is the personal experience of border crossing the contributors bring to their work, although they develop their perspectives in a variety of ways. Based on the primary focus of the essays, they are grouped under the following categories: biblical, theological, and pedagogical. Four of the essays have a distinct biblical focus. The needs of the growing immigrant communities and the need for a just and comprehensive reform of immigration policies prompt Jean-Pierre Ruiz to take a closer look at the biblical imperatives often invoked in some of the documents of the Roman Catholic Church. He uses the border crossing experience of Abram and Sarai from Genesis 12 as an example of reading *with* people on the move. Then Monica Melanchthon offers interesting insights into cross-cultural hermeneutics through an intertextual reading of the story of the Samaritan woman (John 4) with the life and poems of Akkamahadevi of the Virasaiva movement in India of the twelfth century, along with Melanchthon's own experience as the third text.

Charles Amjad-Ali's essay highlights the multilevel cross-border communication in the story of the conversion of Cornelius in Acts 10. He draws particular attention to the colonial or imperial setting of the story. Archie C. C. Lee critiques the border-crossing experience of Li Rongfang (Li Jung-fang, 1887–1965), the first Chinese biblical scholar to be trained in the West. Li Rongfang's interpretation of the Bible in the context of the cultural and political upheavals of the early 1900s in China come under close scrutiny. Lee's focus on this aspect is more than a mere co-incidence as the year 2007 marks the two hundredth anniversary of the first Protestant mission to China. Lee views the translation, presentation, reception, and interpretation of the Bible as a border-crossing experience of significant import within the framework of the colonial missions.

Two essays have a distinctly theological focus. Thomas Thangaraj's essay views boundary crossing as a way of translating theology into theological practice. Using phases from his own theological journey, he argues that when we cross boundaries, whether cultural, linguistic, religious, or musical, we are engaged in theological practice. Kwok Pui-lan proposes "border passage" as an alternative term for border crossing to bring out the ongoing nature of border-negotiating experience. She explores the implications of the sense of place and shape of border passage for contemporary theological reflection.

All of the contributors to this volume have been negotiating multiple boundaries primarily within the academic setting. It is fitting that the pedagogical implications of border crossings are raised in this connection. Two of the essays address this aspect. Musa Dube's essay issues a stirring challenge for curricular transformation in theological studies. Drawing upon her experiences in very diverse educational settings, Dube shows how theological programs and curricula are often predicated upon and circumscribed within the colonial boundaries. Wesley Ariarajah shares "his personal story of hermeneutical experience" as an educator in a theological institution in the United States and shows how the study of scripture, its authority, and its use in other religious traditions brings about transformation in students' attitude toward the Bible.

Finally, a collection devoted to cross-cultural hermeneutics would be incomplete without input from the one who has contributed so much to this area of study. Within a short span of time, the works of R. S. Sugirtharajah have made a significant impact on cross-cultural hermeneutics in general and postcolonial studies in particular. I am grateful to Sugi for contributing to this volume through the interview with his thoughtful reflections and insightful remarks.

Imperfections notwithstanding, my hope is that this small collection furthers the discussion on cross-cultural hermeneutics by focusing on the diasporic interpreters and their border-crossing experiences. The issues raised and insights gained here may find wider application as people appropriate the metaphor of border crossing in their own specific ways. I realize many would have liked to be part of this project honoring Sugi. Due to time constraints, this was not possible. I wish to thank all the contributors for their essays and particularly for being able to work with a tight schedule. My thanks also go to Orbis Books for its enthusiastic support of this project and in particular to Susan Perry, staff editor, for her support, counsel, and guidance.

Notes

1. Arnold E. Davidson, Priscilla L. Walton, and Jennifer Andrews, *Border Crossings: Thomas King's Cultural Inversions* (Toronto: University of Toronto Press, 2003), 15.

2. Homi Bhabha, "Introduction: Narrating the Nation," in *Nation and Narration,* ed. Homi Bhabha (London: Routledge, 1990), 4.

3. Davidson, Walton, and Andrews, *Border Crossings,* 17.

4. Henry Giroux, *Border Crossings: Cultural Workers and the Politics of Education* (New York and London: Routledge, 1992), 27.

5. Ibid., 27.

6. Ibid., 28.

7. Daniel P. Liston and Kenneth M. Zeichner, *Culture and Teaching* (Mahwah, NJ: Lawrence Erlbaum Associates, 1996), 1.

8. Lee Anne Bell, "Theoretical Foundations for Social Justice Education," in *Teaching for Diversity and Social Justice,* ed. Marianne Adams, Lee Anne Bell, and Pat Griffin (New York: Routledge, 1997), 9.

9. David Lusted, "Why Pedagogy?" *Screen* 27, no. 5 (1986): 2.

10. Liston and Zeichner, *Culture and Teaching,* xvii.

11. Ibid.

12. Ian Cook, "Nothing can ever be the case of 'us' and 'them' again: Exploring the Politics of Difference Through Border Pedagogy and Student Journal Writing," *Journal of Geography in Higher Education* 24 (2000): 14.

13. Ibid.

14. Ibid., 15.

15. Henry Giroux, "Democracy and the Discourse of Cultural Difference: Towards a Politics of Border Pedagogy," *British Journal of Sociology of Education* 12, no. 4 (1991): 512.

16. Henry Giroux, *Pedagogy and the Politics of Hope* (Boulder, CO: Westview Press, 1997), 147.

17. Ibid.

18. Ibid.

19. Ibid.

20. Ibid., 148.

21. Ibid., 147.

22. Ibid., 148.

23. Ibid.

24. Ibid.

25. Ibid., 160.

26. Michel Foucault, *Language, Counter-Memory, Practice: Selected Essays and Interviews,* ed. G. Gordon (Ithaca, NY: Cornell University Press, 1977), 163–64.

27. Bruce J. Smith, *Politics and Remembrance* (Princeton: Princeton University Press, 1985), 15–16.

28. Giroux, *Pedagogy and the Politics of Hope,* 155.

29. Ibid., 156.

30. Ibid., 157.

31. Lusted, "Why Pedagogy?" 10.

PART ONE

BIBLICAL PERSPECTIVES

1

ABRAM AND SARAI CROSS THE BORDER

Reading Genesis 12:10–20
with People on the Move

Jean-Pierre Ruiz

A postcolonial critic's role is not limited simply to textual dealings or literary concerns. Postcolonial hermeneutics has to be a pragmatic engagement, an engagement in which praxis is not an extra option or a subsidiary enterprise taken in the aftermath of judicious decon-struction and reconstruction of the texts. Rather, this praxeological involvement is there from the outset of the hermeneutical process, informing and contesting the whole procedure. If we neglect this, we may become ridiculous figures like the Lavatrie Alltheorie portrayed in Rukun Advani's novel Beethoven among the Cows. *In the longest chapter of the book, entitled "S/he, or A Postmodern Chapter on Gender and Identity," Lavatrie Alltheorie is described as a "Post-modern theoretician, boa deconstructor, discourse analyst, post-structural critic, feminist historian of subalternity, colonialism and gender." A diasporic Indian academic, she offers courses to packed audiences of white students on "the semiology of Deconstruction and the Deconstruction of semiology." The danger is that we will be seen as deliberately using catchphrases and buzzwords as a form of posture and power play. As Arun Mukherjee says, it is not enough to fight the colonizer with the "textual weapons of irony and parody." If we do so, we may, like Lavatrie Alltheorie, become renowned for "specialization in Complete Bunkum."* —R. S. Sugirtharajah[1]

Sugirtharajah's wise and witty words of caution often echo in this Nuyor-
ican biblical scholar's mind. Years ago, I spent more than a few sleepless
nights during the last weeks of my work as parochial vicar at the Roman
Catholic Church of Our Lady of Loreto in the East New York section
of Brooklyn, wondering whether I was doing the right thing by leaving
inner-city ministry in that Latino/a and African American community
to return to Rome for a doctoral degree in biblical studies. I had to
ask myself over and over again whether I was escaping from the daily
grind of *la lucha* into the pages of the Bible. Sugirtharajah insists: "The
task of postcolonialism is to insure that the yearnings of the poor take
precedence over the interests of the affluent; that the emancipation of the
subjugated has primacy over the freedom of the powerful; and that the
participation of the marginalized takes priority over the perpetuation of
a system which systematically excludes them."[2]

This imperative prodded my conscience over and over again when I
attended a meeting in Miami that brought together a group of Latino/a
biblical scholars and pastoral agents, Roman Catholic and Protestant,
to explore the possibility of producing a *Biblia del Inmigrante*. This
was to have been a Spanish translation of the Bible intended to provide
spiritual sustenance for the many thousands of Latin Americans who
cross the border from Mexico to the United States, a compact volume
that would be available at little or no cost on both sides of the border.
Besides study helps and explanatory material, the projected *Biblia del
Inmigrante* was to include practical information that would be useful for
Spanish-speaking immigrants making their way in the United States. The
project did not make it very far, for the proposed *Biblia del Inmigrante*
was never published, and perhaps it is just as well, for reading the Bible
at the border is no simple matter. Indeed, such reading raises as many
vexing questions as it provides answers.

As I frame these reflections that were set in motion by my involvement
as a consultant to that well-intentioned project, I turn first of all to
several key statements on immigration issued over the last several years
by the leadership of my own Roman Catholic faith community, to see
the ways in which these statements appeal to texts from the Hebrew
Bible. I am especially interested in the ways in which these documents
make reference to texts from the Hebrew Bible to argue in favor of just
and comprehensive reforms of immigration policies, and to ground the
church's efforts to serve the needs of the growing immigrant community.

I then turn from biblical imperatives to a narrative, a provocative and challenging text that I offer as a case study for reading *with* people on the move, a text that provides a mirror from antiquity to the challenges that immigrants and refugees continue to face.[3]

Biblical Imperatives and the World in Front of the Text

In May of 2004, the Vatican's Pontifical Council for Migrants and Refugees published an instruction entitled *Erga migrantes caritas Christi,* "The Love of Christ towards Migrants."[4] That instruction was addressed mainly to Catholic pastoral agents entrusted with the responsibility of attending to the needs of migrants and refugees. The purpose was to consider the pressing reality of people on the move — some two hundred million around the world — and to formulate effective pastoral strategies for meeting their needs. After an introduction that sketches "The Migration Phenomenon Today" (*Erga migrantes* 1–11), Part One of the instruction, "Migration, Sign of the Times and Concern for the Church" (*Erga migrantes* 12–32), begins with a treatment of "Migration as Seen with the Eyes of Faith" (*Erga migrantes* 12–13), which suggests that migration should be seen:

> in the light of those biblical events that mark the phases of humanity's arduous journey towards the birth of a people without discrimination or frontiers, depository of God's gift for all nations and open to man's eternal vocation. Faith perceives in it the journey of the Patriarchs, sustained by the promise as they moved towards the future homeland, and that of the Hebrews, freed from slavery, as they crossed the Red Sea in the Exodus, that formed the People of the Covenant. Again, in a certain sense, faith finds in migration an exile, in which every goal reached in fact is relative. In migration faith discovers once more the <u>universal</u> message of the prophets, who denounce discrimination, oppression, deportation, dispersion and persecution as contrary to God's plan. At the same time they proclaim salvation for all, witnessing even in the chaotic events and contradictions of human history, that God continues to work out his plan of salvation until all things are brought together in Christ (cf. Eph 1:10). (*Erga migrantes* 13)

The instruction invites believers to see in the present realities of people on the move not an obstacle to the accomplishment of God's will but an unfolding of God's purposes "even in the chaotic events and contradictions of human history." It is under the heading of "Migration and the History of Salvation" that the instruction very briefly considers migration in the Hebrew Bible:

> Israel traced its origins back to Abraham, who in obedience to God's call left his home and went to a foreign land, taking with him the divine Promise that he would become the father "of a great nation" (Gn 12:1–2). Jacob, a wandering Aramean, "went down into Egypt with a small household and lived there as an alien. But there he became a nation, great, strong and numerous" (Dt 26:5). After its long servitude in Egypt Israel received its solemn investiture as the "People of God" during its forty-year "Exodus" through the desert. The hard test of migration and deportation is therefore fundamental to the story of the chosen people in view of the salvation of all peoples: Israel knew the return from exile (cf. Is 42:6–7; 49:5). With these memories it could take new heart in its trust in God, even in the darkest moments of its history (Ps 105 [104]: 12–15; Ps 106 [105]: 45–47).With regard to the foreigner living in the country, the Law enjoins the same commandment on Israel as applies to "the children of your people" (Lv 19:18), that is, "you must . . . love him as yourself" (Lv 19:34). (*Erga migrantes* 14)

It is clearly not the intention of this instruction to provide a comprehensive survey of how the Hebrew Bible deals with immigrants, refugees, and other people on the move. It does seek to underscore Israel's story as the story of a people on the move: "The hard test of migration and deportation is therefore fundamental to the story of the chosen people." This story begins with Abraham, whom God commands: "Go from your country and your kindred and your father's house to the land that I will show you" (Gn 12:1). The subsequent biblical citations in this paragraph of the Vatican instruction include a reference to Deuteronomy 26:1–11, the offering of firstfruits to be made by those who have settled in the land.[5] This offering was to be accompanied by the response:

> A wandering Aramean was my ancestor; he went down into Egypt and lived there as an alien, few in number, and there he became a

great nation, mighty and populous. When the Egyptians treated us harshly and afflicted us, by imposing hard labor on us, we cried to the Lord, the God of our ancestors; the Lord heard our voice and saw our affliction, our toil, and our oppression. The Lord brought us out of Egypt with a mighty hand and an outstretched arm, with a terrifying display of power, and with signs and wonders; and he brought us into this place and gave us this land, a land flowing with milk and honey (Dt 26:5–9).[6]

It is this experience of living as aliens in Egypt that is the ground of solidarity on which the precepts of the Holiness Code calls Israel to treat aliens, in the last biblical citation noted in *Erga migrantes* 14, that is, Leviticus 19:34: "The alien who resides with you shall be to you as the citizen among you; you shall love the alien as yourself, for you were aliens in the land of Egypt: I am the LORD your God."

In 2003, a year before the Pontifical Council for Migrants and Refugees published *Erga migrantes caritas Christi,* the Roman Catholic bishops of Mexico and the United States published a joint pastoral letter entitled, *Strangers No Longer: Together on the Journey of Hope,* a symbolic and substantive contribution to the discussion on immigration from Latin America into the United States. The bishops explained:

We speak as two episcopal conferences but as one Church, united in the view that migration between our two nations is necessary and beneficial. At the same time, some aspects of the migrant experience are far from the vision of the Kingdom of God that Jesus proclaimed: many persons who seek to migrate are suffering, and, in some cases, tragically dying; human rights are abused; families are kept apart; and racist and xenophobic attitudes remain.[7]

Here too, as in the subsequent Vatican instruction, the bishops take a moment to present reflections on "Migration in the Light of the Word of God," with two paragraphs devoted to migration in the Old Testament (nos. 24 and 25) and two paragraphs to the New Testament (nos. 26 and 27). With regard to people on the move in the Old Testament, the bishops observed:

Even in the harsh stories of migration, God is present, revealing himself. Abraham stepped out in faith to respond to God's call (Gn 12:1). He and Sarah extended bounteous hospitality to three strangers who were actually a manifestation of the Lord, and this became a paradigm for the response to strangers of Abraham's descendants. The grace of God even broke through situations of sin in the forced migration of the children of Jacob: Joseph, sold into slavery, eventually became the savior of his family (Gn 37:45) — a type of Jesus, who, betrayed by a friend for thirty pieces of silver, saves the human family.

The key events in the history of the Chosen People of enslavement by the Egyptians and of liberation by God led to commandments regarding strangers (Ex 23:9; Lv 19:33). Israel's conduct with the stranger is both an imitation of God and the primary, specific Old Testament manifestation of the great commandment to love one's neighbor: "For the Lord, your God, is the . . . Lord of lords, the great God, mighty and awesome, who has no favorites, accepts no bribes, who executes justice for the orphan and widow, and befriends the alien, feeding and clothing him. So you, too, must befriend the alien, for you were once aliens yourselves in the land of Egypt" (Dt 10:17–19). For the Israelites, these injunctions were not only personal exhortations: the welcome and care of the alien were structured into their gleaning and tithing laws (Lv 19:9–10; Dt 14:28–29).[8]

In an era of rampant human trafficking, the Joseph story takes on a special poignancy. Likewise, in an era of ever increasing xenophobia and intolerance toward undocumented immigrants, the precepts of Leviticus and Deuteronomy should stir the consciences of those who themselves "were once aliens," whether a generation ago or centuries ago.[9] More recently, the Roman Catholic bishops of Arizona referred to the very same texts (Deuteronomy 10 and Leviticus 19) in their own pastoral letter on migration, "You Welcomed Me," addressing themselves to their fellow Arizonans, residents of a state that "has become the focal point of the immigration debate in recent years,"[10] and where Governor Janet Napolitano vetoed a bill passed by the Arizona legislature that would have criminalized undocumented immigrants in her state.

There can be no doubt that the Roman Catholic bishops of the United States have taken a high profile stance in the current public policy debate in the United States regarding immigration reform, with none more prominent than the archbishop of Los Angeles, Cardinal Roger Mahony, who at the beginning of Lent 2006 made clear his opposition to the Border Protection, Anti-Terrorism and Illegal Immigration Control Act (H.R. 4437) then being debated by the House of Representatives.[11] Mahony made equally clear his intention to instruct the priests of the archdiocese to disobey the law inasmuch as its provisions called for service providers (not excluding religious workers) to ascertain the immigration status of their clients. This courageous stance received applause from such unexpected quarters as the *New York Times,* where the lead editorial of the March 3, 2006, issue carried the headline, "The Gospel vs. H.R.4437." The editorial went on to praise what it called Mahony's "declaration of solidarity with illegal immigrants":

> It has been a long time since this country heard a call to organized lawbreaking on this big a scale. . . . If current efforts in Congress make it a felony to shield or offer support to illegal immigrants, Cardinal Mahony said, he will instruct his priests — and faithful lay Catholics — to defy the law. . . . Cardinal Mahony's declaration of solidarity with illegal immigrants, for whom Lent is every day, is a startling call to civil disobedience, as courageous as it is timely. We hope it forestalls the day when works of mercy become a federal crime.[12]

Not everyone was moved to applaud. In the pages of the *National Review,* George Neumayr wrote about Cardinal Mahony's stance: "Contrary to his faux-pious rhetoric, he is speaking not for the Catholic Church but for himself, using, in a textbook example of clericalism, the prestige and trappings of his episcopal office to advance nothing more than his personal opinion in favor of open borders."[13] Congressional Representative Peter King, the co-sponsor of H.R. 4437, called for his church's bishops to stay out of politics and "spend more time protecting little boys from pedophile priests." A self-confessed "blue collar Catholic," King mused about his opposition to the church's stance on immigration: "It's quite possible this could end up helping me politically. Maybe it shows that God's on my side."[14] This is the same Peter King who in 2004, according to *Newsday* reporter Glenn Thrush, "dismissed the Vatican's criticism of the U.S. military's human rights abuses at Iraq's Abu Ghraib prison, saying they were 'nothing compared to what nuns and priests did to Catholic kids for decades.' "[15] It is unmistakably clear that there is still a lot of preaching to the choir that needs to take place (since the "choir" includes Catholics like Peter King and Minuteman co-founder Jim Gilchrist), that many more Catholic Christians need to take to heart their church's embrace of the imperative of Leviticus 19:34: "The alien who resides with you shall be to you as the citizen among you; you shall love the alien as yourself, for you were aliens in the land of Egypt: I am the LORD your God."

On the basis of statements from Rome and from leaders in the United States, it is clear that the Catholic Church's stance on immigration reform has deep roots in the biblical imperatives that flow from Israel's consciousness as a people "who were once aliens in the land of Egypt." In the world in front of the biblical text, that ethical consciousness is shaped by centuries-long patterns of immigration to the United States, constituted as a "nation of immigrants" with a national mythology that continues to tap into biblical narratives for its language and its substance.[16] Thus, solidarity with recently arrived immigrants that is called for by church leaders is framed as fitting recognition of a shared heritage of migration at a greater or lesser distance in time. It must be noted, though, that the statements by church leadership regarding immigration reform too often fall into the trap of speaking about immigrants — especially the undocumented — in the third person plural, speaking about "them" in ways that do not take account of the fact that Hispanics (including both Latin American immigrants and U.S.-born Latinas/os) represent 71 percent of the U.S. Catholic population growth since 1960, that some 39 percent of Roman Catholics in the United States are of Latin American origin (Latin American immigrants and U.S.-born Latinas/os), and that more than 20 percent of Roman Catholic parishes in the United States are majority Latino/a.[17] When church leadership comes to reckon with statistics like these, there can be no doubt that "they" are "us"[18] and that the solidarity they call for is not only *ad extra* and at a distance, but *ad intra* as well. From this emerges the important insight that dealing with the Bible and immigrants calls us to engage not only in reading *about* immigrants but also in reading *as* immigrants and reading *with* immigrants.

People on the Move in the Hebrew Bible

Dianne Bergant explains that "two Hebrew words are used by the biblical authors to distinguish those who belong to other nations. Though the words are sometimes used interchangeably, *nokri* usually refers to transient foreigners and *ger* to sojourners or resident aliens."[19] Francisco García-Treto suggests:

> If we were to summarize in a single phrase the clear thesis of these biblical traditions [regarding migration], it would be, simply, that the *ger* is protected by Yahweh. The ancient Hebrew Tradition is clearly different from the xenophobic attitudes that were prevalent in antiquity.... The *ger*, the alien who lives among the people of Israel, could have been completely deprived of dignity and even of the most basic right to justice, since the *ger* lacked the two traditional elements that, at the purely human level, were the foundation of dignity and right in Israel: hereditary property, and the protection of family and kinship. The biblical tradition, however, surprises us by including the *ger* as the object of a particular predilection on Yahweh's part, and therefore to be included, jointly with the native, in the rites that expressed the community's solidarity, as well as among those to whom the law grants a special protection.[20]

Commenting on García-Treto's observations, Justo González notes that "the *ger* even serves a specific religious function in Israel, reminding the people that Israel too was alien in the land of Egypt, and remains forever alien in a land that ultimately belongs only to God."[21] According to García-Treto,

> The biblical tradition... reiterates that Israel not only was, but still is, an "alien" people. Solidarity with the dispossessed is not only an external attitude, but the deepest reality of Israel's existence as people of Yahweh. References such as Deuteronomy 28:8 remind Israel that it too was a *ger* in Egypt, but even more relevant are others such as the one in Leviticus 25:23, where Yahweh admonishes the people: "The land shall not be sold in perpetuity, for the land is mine; with me you are but aliens and tenants."[22]

This dynamic suggests that the reading strategy I am offering, that is, the practice of not only reading *about* immigrants but also reading *as* immigrants and reading *with* immigrants holds promise. As we proceed, I would like to offer a case study for the practice of reading *as* immigrants and reading *with* immigrants. The text I offer for consideration is Genesis 12:10–20, the episode in the patriarchal narrative where a famine in Canaan forces Abram to seek refuge as a resident alien in Egypt (Gn 12:10: "Now there was a famine in the land. So Abram went down to Egypt to reside there as an alien, for the famine was severe in the land"). In effect Abram became a temporary economic migrant. The selection of this text as a case study does not imply either that this text is especially appropriate for reading *with* twenty-first-century people on the move, or that it ought to be understood as prescriptive or normative for the conduct of twenty-first-century people on the move. Neither do I mean to suggest that this text furnishes an appropriate model for navigating the challenges of living in a land that is not one's own — quite the contrary![23] Yet by selecting this text as a case study I *do* mean to suggest that the characterization of people on the move in the Hebrew Bible is substantially more complex and substantially more nuanced than one might be led to believe on the basis of the somewhat limited range of texts from the Hebrew Bible that are referenced in recent official Roman Catholic documents regarding migrants and refugees. To be sure, the biblical imperatives that find a place in these documents to renew in the present-day the ancient call for justice toward migrants ring deeply true.[24] At the same time, the range of biblical narratives involving characters who are people on the move testifies to the pervasiveness across history of the challenges of moving across borders, and to the difficulty of the ethical choices and tactical decisions people make in order to survive in lands far from their own.

Abram and Sarai Cross the Border:
Genesis 12:10–20

Now there was a famine in the land. So Abram went down to Egypt to reside there as an alien, for the famine was severe in the land. When he was about to enter Egypt, he said to his wife Sarai, "I know well that you are a woman beautiful in appearance; and when the Egyptians see you, they will say, 'This is his wife'; then they will kill me, but they will let you live. Say you are my sister, so that it may go well with me because of you, and that my life may be spared on your account." When Abram entered Egypt the Egyptians saw that the woman was very beautiful. When the officials of Pharaoh saw her, they praised her to Pharaoh. And the woman was taken into Pharaoh's house. And for her sake he dealt well with Abram; and he had sheep, oxen, male donkeys, male and female slaves, female donkeys, and camels. But the LORD afflicted Pharaoh and his house with great plagues because of Sarai, Abram's wife. So Pharaoh called Abram, and said, "What is this you have done to me? Why did you not tell me that she was your wife? Why did you say, 'She is my sister,' so that I took her for my wife? Now then, here is your wife, take her, and be gone." And Pharaoh gave his men orders concerning him; and they set him on the way, with his wife and all that he had.

Robert Alter identifies this text as a type scene, for it is one of the three instances in Genesis in which "a patriarch is driven by famine to a southern region where he pretends that his wife is his sister, narrowly avoids a violation of the conjugal bond by the local ruler, and is sent away with gifts."[25] Abram and Sarai are involved in two such scenes, Genesis 12:10–20 and 20:1–18, and Isaac and Rebekah in Genesis 26:1–16. Susan Niditch writes of these wife/sister tales:

Three times in Genesis when a patriarch and his wife are "sojourn-ing" — traveling as resident aliens — in a foreign land, the ruler of the country is told that the wife is a sister of the patriarch. In two versions he takes her to be his own woman, and each time the couple is eventually found out. Despite the similarities, the three stories possess quite different nuances and voices. It is assumed in all three versions that a brother has more power to exchange his sister than a husband his wife. The patriarchs are portrayed as as-suming that the foreigners would not hesitate to kill a husband in order to get a woman but that they would engage in normal marital exchange with a brother. The story that makes the most sense in a crass, male-centered way is the version in 12:10–20, where it is clear that Abram has more to gain as the brother of an unmarried, protected woman than as the husband of a "used" one.[26]

I will focus on the first of these scenes, Genesis 12:10–20.[27] Gordon Wenham points out the clearly concentric structure of the tale:

A   Exposition: Entry (v. 10)
   B   First Scene: Abram's Speech (vv. 10–13)
      C   Second Scene: The Ruse at Work (vv. 14–16)
   B¹ Third Scene: Pharaoh's Speech (vv. 17–19)
A¹ Conclusion: Exit (v. 20)[28]

From the very outset of the story, it is clear that Abram and Sarai are economic refugees from Canaan, crossing the border into Egypt to escape a deadly famine. The concentric structure of verse 10 frames Abram's journeying to Egypt to live there as a resident alien between mentions of the famine in the land. This is the second explicit reference to the severity of the famine. The mention of Abram's journey into Egypt comes abruptly after the vision at Shechem described in 12:7: "Then the Lord appeared to Abram, and said, 'To your offspring I will give this land.' So he built there an altar to the Lord, who had appeared to him." His intention to sojourn in Egypt as a resident alien as a result of the famine raises considerable doubt, generating significant narrative tension that is resolved only at the conclusion of the story. Having left his homeland in pursuit of God's promise, would he have his hopes dashed by the very barrenness of a land that would prove more a curse than a blessing? Would he end his days as an alien sojourning in a land far from his own?

It is not unimportant for the development of the narrative that Abram gives voice to his fears about the dangers that lie ahead just as he is about to cross into Egyptian territory. As Wenham writes,

> Escaping the danger of famine in Canaan, Abram fears that in Egypt he will run another sort of risk. As an immigrant there he would lack the support and protection afforded by the wider family network. The danger of immigrants being exploited is frequently harped on in the law, as, for example, in Exodus 22:20 (21) and 23:9. Why Abram should have felt secure in Canaan but exposed in Egypt is not explained, though of course strange environments often do give rise to unfounded fears.[29]

To the twenty-first-century interpreters who read *as* and *with* immigrants, there is nothing unfounded at all about the fears involved in border crossings. To those who cross the border between Mexico and the United States, the physical dangers are altogether terrifying, and the fear of deportation once across the border is no less preoccupying. Claus Westermann successfully sketches the geopolitical dimensions of such perils — albeit in another era and another place — describing yet another instance of well-founded fear elsewhere in Genesis:

> As one who has to beg for food, Abraham has no rights. We meet this same feeling, of being delivered to a far superior power without protection, once more in the case of Joseph's brothers on their way down to Egypt. Real experience lies behind this — that of a small group confronted by a superpower. The mighty colossus engenders the feeling of utter powerlessness on the part of the lesser one. It is in this situation in the ancient world that the ruse everywhere has its place. The ruse is the only weapon left for the powerless given over to the mighty.[30]

Giving voice to his fear about the danger he will face when they enter Egyptian territory, Abram asks Sarai to say that she is his sister, "so that it may go well with me because of you, and that my life may be spared on your account" (v. 13). For her part, Sarai says nothing at this point, nor do we hear her voice at any point in the story. In verse 20, the pharaoh addresses Abram to ask, "Why did you say, 'She is my sister,' so that I took her for my wife?" Yet Niditch suggests that Abram and Sarai are actually "co-tricksters," pointing out that Abram uses "coaxing language" in his request, "Please say you are my sister." Niditch warns:

> This is no woman-affirming tale. Sarai is an exchange item to be traded for wealth. She is shown as accepting this role, as are all the women in Genesis. She and Abram play out their roles in a particular social structure, but do so as marginals. Facing famine in their own land, they flee to Egypt, where they have insecure status. There they use deception to improve their situation at the expense of those who have authority over them.[31]

The intertwined dynamics of power and gender that are at work in Sarai's silent compliance with Abram's request come full circle in the story's second speech, where it is Abram who is reduced to silence, giving no response to the pharaoh's question, "Why did you say, 'She is my sister,' so that I took her for my wife?" (v. 20). Yet the pharaoh sends Abram away with all his possessions — his newly acquired wealth and his wife besides — and the patriarch leaves Egypt and returns "to the place where his tent had been at the beginning, between Bethel and Ai, to the place where he had made an altar at the first; and there Abram called on the name of the Lord" (13:3). Genesis 13:3 forms an inclusion with 13:8–9, framing the story of Abraham as a transnational temporary migrant from Canaan to Egypt and back again.

Nahum Sarna prefers to call the story in Genesis 12:10–20 "The Kidnapping of Sarah," suggesting that the pharaoh's officials "carry her off to the royal palace. Only divine intervention protects her honor and she returns to her husband unviolated."[32] It is evident from verse 16 that what happened was anything but a kidnapping. As Niditch points out, Sarai was an "exchange item to be traded for wealth."[33] Happily-ever-after ending or not, this episode in the Abraham story is deeply disturbing. Sarna writes:

> The biblical heroes are not portrayed as demigods or perfect human beings. They are mortals of flesh and blood, subject to the same temptations and possessed of the same frailties as are all other human beings. Abram, the man of implicit faith in God's word, is fearful of the evil of which people are capable. In order to save his own life, he appears to place his wife's honor in jeopardy through misrepresentation of their relationship. Sarai's collusion may be looked upon as an act of self-sacrifice on behalf of her husband — but how is Abram's conduct to be judged? Ramban comments as follows: "Know that our father Abraham inadvertently committed a great sin by placing his virtuous wife in a compromising situation because of his fear of being killed. He should have trusted in God to save him, his wife and all he had, for God has the power to help and to save."[34]

By turns, commentators either lament Abram's failure to trust in God, or they point to the version of the story in Genesis 26 to suggest that Abram was actually telling the truth by having Sarai identified as his sister (Gn 26:12: "she is indeed my sister, the daughter of my father but not the daughter of my mother; and she became my wife."). Some of the commentators who favor the latter option then invoke some indirect evidence for practices in surrounding cultures that sanctioned some sort of endogamous marriage to one's sister.[35] Whether or not she was complicit in Abram's ruse, Sarai finds herself doubly victimized by powerful males in this story: first by her own husband, whose fear and desire for self-preservation take priority over her welfare, and second by the pharaoh, the foreign sovereign whose attendants acquire her for their master's house in a transaction in which Abram receives far more live-stock than he loses by surrendering Sarai: "sheep, oxen, male donkeys, male and female slaves, female donkeys, and camels" (Gn 12:16). In the end, Abram the trickster leaves Egypt safe and sound, with all of his newly acquired wealth *and* Sarai as well (Gn 12:20).

Conclusion

What happens when we read about Sarai's experience of crossing the border into Egypt along with Gloria Anzaldúa? Anzaldúa writes the following about what faces those who cross the border between the United States and Mexico:

Living in a no-man's borderland, caught between being treated as criminals and being able to eat, between resistance and deportation, the illegal refugees are some of the poorest and the most exploited of any people in the U.S. It is illegal for Mexicans to work without green cards. But big farming combines, farm bosses and smugglers who bring them in to make money off the "wetbacks'" labor — they don't have to pay federal minimum wages, or ensure adequate housing or sanitary conditions.

The Mexican woman is especially at risk. Often the *coyote* (smuggler) doesn't feed her for days or let her go to the bathroom. Often he rapes her or sells her into prostitution. She cannot call on county or state health or economic resources because she doesn't know English and she fears deportation. American employers are quick to take advantage of her helplessness. She can't go home. She's sold her house, her furniture, borrowed from her friends to pay the *coyote* who charges her four or five thousand dollars to smuggle her to Chicago. She may work as a live-in maid for a white, Chicano or Latino household for as little as $15 a week. Or work in the garment industry, do hotel work. Isolated and worried about her family back home, afraid of getting caught and deported, living with as many as fifteen people in one room, the *mexicana* suffers serious health problems. *Se enferma de los nervios, de alta presión.*

La mujer, la mujer indocumentada, is doubly threatened in this country. Not only does she have to contend with sexual violence, but like all women, she is prey to a sense of physical helplessness. As a refugee, she leaves the familiar and safe home-ground to venture into unknown and possibly dangerous terrain.

> This is her home
> This thin edge of
> barbwire.[36]

What happens when we read Genesis 12:10–20 *with* women who have crossed the border from Mexico into the United States? The very first words we hear from the mouth of the border-crosser Abram are the words of fear he whispers to his wife in Genesis 12:11–13, and it is Sarai who becomes the victim of her husband's fear when that fear is the force that keeps him from seeing her as spouse or as sister but as no more than livestock that can assure him a prosperous future in spite of famine. For the twenty-first-century border crossers, there is ample cause for fear. Thousands have died in the years since the Clinton administration launched Operation Gatekeeper to seal the border between Tijuana and San Diego.[37] A 2006 report issued by the United States Government Accountability Office found that "since 1995, the number of border-crossing deaths increased and by 2005 had more than doubled," and "the annual number of border-crossing deaths increased from 241 in 1999 to a total of 472 deaths recorded in 2005." Further, "deaths among women increased from 9 percent of all deaths in 1998 to 21 percent of all deaths in 2005."[38]

The moral clarity of the regulations in the Hebrew Bible regarding the treatment of aliens becomes considerably more muddled as these aliens themselves become implicated in the tensions between disclosure and non-disclosure, between truth and trickery that are essential to survival in the borderlands, between life and death at the barbed wire boundary where the collateral damage is considerable and where the most vulnerable also become the most expendable. The stories of people on the move in the Hebrew Bible are colored not in simple black and white, but in subtle and complex shades. In the world in front of the text, the stories of people on the move across the border between Mexico and the United States in the twenty-first century are stories too often written in their own sweat and blood. For the responsible reader of the Bible, who recognizes with Sugirtharajah that "postcolonial hermeneutics has to be a pragmatic engagement, an engagement in which praxis is not an extra option or a subsidiary enterprise taken in the aftermath of judicious deconstruction and reconstruction of the texts," there must be no flight from these stories into the pages of the ancient text.[39]

Notes

1. "A Postcolonial Exploration of Collusion and Construction in Biblical Interpretation," in *The Postcolonial Bible,* ed. R. S. Sugirtharajah, The Bible and Postcolonialism 1 (Sheffield: Sheffield Academic Press, 1998), 113–14. The citation references found in the body of the original text are omitted here.

2. Ibid., 113.

3. On "reading with" as a hermeneutical stance, see Fernando F. Segovia, "Reading Across: Intercultural Criticism and Textual Posture," in *Interpreting beyond Borders,* ed. Fernando F. Segovia, The Bible and Postcolonialism 3 (Sheffield: Sheffield Academic Press, 2000), 68–72, a presentation and analysis of the work of Gerald West.

4. Hereafter *Erga migrantes.* Available online at the Vatican's Internet site: *vatican.mondosearch.com/search.aspxat* (accessed April 16, 2007).

5. See Aelred Cody, O.S.B., " 'Little Historical Creed' or 'Little Historical Anamnesis,' " *Catholic Biblical Quarterly* 68 (2006): 1–10.

6. Except as noted, biblical translations into English are from the New Revised Standard Version.

7. United States Conference of Catholic Bishops and Conferencia del Episcopado Mexicano, *Strangers No Longer: Together on the Journey of Hope,* a pastoral letter concerning migration from the Catholic bishops of Mexico and the United States (Washington, DC: United States Conference of Catholic Bishops, 2003), available on the Internet at *www.usccb.org/mrs/stranger.shtml* (accessed April 16, 2007).

8. *Strangers No Longer,* nos. 24–25. The citation "Gn 37:45" is incorrect; there is no verse 45 in Genesis 37. The citation should probably read Genesis 37–45, the chapters that contain the Joseph story.

9. The *New York Times* reports that as Georgia governor Sonny Perdue signed into law the Georgia Security and Immigration Compliance Act, a harsh anti-immigrant measure, "The crowd waved American flags and cheered as State Representative Melvin Everson, a black Republican in the House, denounced illegal immigration as a cancer. 'The last time I checked,' Mr. Everson said, 'America was the land of English, not Spanish' " (*New York Times,* April 18, 2006, A16).

10. Gerald Kicanas, Thomas Olmsted, Donald Pelotte, and William Skurla, "You Welcomed Me: Migration Pastoral Letter," *Origins* 35, no. 29 (January 5, 2006): 477–83. In reflecting on the biblical foundations of the church's response to the situation of people on the move, the Arizona bishops draw on the November 15, 2000, statement of the U.S. Catholic bishops, *Welcoming the Stranger among Us: Unity in Diversity,* available on the Internet at *www.usccb.org/mrs/unity.shtml#church* (accessed April 16, 2007).

11. See Joe Feuerherd, "Bishops United on Immigration," *National Catholic Reporter,* April 21, 2006. The October 18, 2005, "Interfaith Statement in Support of Comprehensive Immigration Reform," with more than a hundred Jewish, Christian, and Muslim signatories, likewise urged Congress to "enact comprehensive immigration reform legislation that establishes a safe and humane immigration system consistent with our values. Our diverse faith traditions teach us to welcome our brothers and sisters with love and compassion," citing Leviticus 19 as a biblical foundation for such a faith-based stance. This document is available on the Internet at *www.usccb.org/mrs/interfaith.shtml* (accessed April 16, 2007).

12. *New York Times,* March 3, 2006, A22. Cardinal Mahony himself contributed an op-ed piece to the *New York Times,* in which he explained his opposition to H.R. 4437 and his call for just and comprehensive immigration reform. See Roger Mahony, "Called by God to Help," *New York Times,* March 22, 2006, A25.

13. George Neumayr, "Cardinal Sin," *National Review Online* (April 12, 2006). Available online at *www.nationalreview.com/comment/neumayr200604120719.asp* (accessed April 16, 2007).

14. Glenn Thrush, "LI Congressman Takes a Controversial Stance," *Newsday* April 2, 2006.

15. Ibid.

16. See United States Conference of Catholic Bishops, *Welcoming the Stranger among Us,* available on the Internet at *www.usccb.org/mrs/unity.shtml* (accessed April 17, 2006). In his March 25, 2006, radio address, President George Bush himself referred to the United States as "a nation of immigrants" and a "nation of laws." Available at *www.whitehouse.gov/news/releases/2006/03/20060325.html* (accessed April 17, 2007). In a speech delivered at a March 27, 2006, naturalization ceremony, President Bush boasted: "Our immigrant heritage has enriched America's history. It continues to shape our society. Each generation of immigrants brings a renewal to our national character and adds vitality to our culture" (*www.whitehouse.gov/news/releases/2006/03/20060327.html;* accessed on April 17, 2007).

17. These statistics are reported on the web page of the Secretariat for Hispanic Affairs of the United States Conference of Catholic Bishops, and they represent the results of pre-2000 surveys. It is entirely likely that these numbers have increased considerably since these data were collected (United States Conference of Catholic Bishops Secretariat for Hispanic Affairs, "Demographics," available on the Internet at *www.usccb.org/hispanicaffairs/demo.shtml#4;* accessed April 17, 2007).

18. For an insightful analysis of "they"/"us" language vis-à-vis church documents regarding the preferential option for the poor, see Carmen M. Nanko, "Justice Crosses the Border: The Preferential Option for the Poor in the United States," in *A Reader in Latina Feminist Theology: Religion and Justice,* ed. María Pilar Aquino, Daisy Machado, and Jeanette Rodriguez (Austin: University of Texas Press, 2002), 177–203, and especially 186–87. Also see Carmen M. Nanko-Fernández, "We Are Not Your Diversity, We Are the Church! Ecclesiological Reflections from the Marginalized Many," in *Perspectivas: Hispanic Theological Initiative Occasional Papers 10* (Fall 2006): 81–117.

19. Dianne Bergant "Ruth: The Migrant Who Saved the People," in *Migration, Religious Experience, and Globalization,* ed. Gioacchino Campese and Pietro Cialella (New York: Center for Migration Studies, 2003), 51.

20. Francisco O. García-Treto, "El Señor guarda a los emigrantes," *Apuntes* 1, no. 4 (Winter 1981): 4, as translated by and cited in Justo L. González, *Santa Biblia: The Bible through Hispanic Eyes* (Nashville: Abingdon, 1996), 94. With regard to xenophobic attitudes in the Bible itself, see Francisco O. García-Treto, "The Lesson of the Gibeonites: A Proposal for Dialogic Attention as a Strategy for Reading the Bible," in *Hispanic/Latino Theology: Challenge and Promise,* ed. Ada María Isasi-Díaz and Fernando F. Segovia (Minneapolis: Fortress, 1996), 73–85.

21. González, *Santa Biblia,* 94.

22. García-Treto, "El Señor guarda a los emigrantes," 6–7, as translated and cited in González, *Santa Biblia,* 94. On Leviticus 25:23, see Jacob Milgrom, *Leviticus 23–27: A New Translation with Introduction and Commentary,* Anchor Bible 3B (New York: Doubleday, 2001), 2183–2191.

23. A variety of other texts might yield equally provocative readings. The book of Ruth, for example, is a text that vividly illustrates the tensions between identity and assimilation, and the difficult and painful decisions that face people on the move. See Laura Donaldson's re-reading of the book of Ruth as a Cherokee woman: "The Sign of Orpah: Reading Ruth through Native Eyes," in *Vernacular Hermeneutics,* ed. R. S. Sugirtharajah, The Bible and Postcolonialism 2 (Sheffield: Sheffield Academic Press, 1999), 20–36.

24. See Luis R. Rivera Rodríguez, "Immigration and the Bible: Comments by a Diasporic Theologian," in *Perspectivas: Hispanic Theological Initiative Occasional Papers* 10 (Fall 2006): 23–36. Also see Harold V. Bennett, *Injustice Made Legal: Deuteronomic Law and the Plight of Widows, Strangers, and Orphans in Ancient Israel* (Grand Rapids: Eerdmans, 2002), and Christiana van Houten, *The Alien in Israelite Law,* JSOTSup 231 (Sheffield: JSOT Press, 1991).

25. Robert Alter, *The Art of Biblical Narrative* (New York: Basic Books, 1981), 49.

26. Susan Niditch, "Genesis," in *The Women's Bible Commentary,* ed. Carol A. Newsom and Sharon H. Ringe (Louisville: Westminster/John Knox Press, 1992), 18.

27. Niditch ("Genesis," 18) provides a clear and concise sketch of the narrative nuances of the three different versions of the tale.

28. Gordon Wenham, *Genesis 1–15,* Word Biblical Commentary 1 (Waco, TX: Word Books, 1987), 286. Wenham identifies C (vv. 14–16) as "Fulfillment of Abram's fears." I suggest instead that the ruse works, inasmuch as verse 16 tells us that for Sarai's sake the pharaoh dealt well with Abram, just as in verse 13 Abram expressed his hope that it would.

29. Wenham, *Genesis 1–15,* 287–88.

30. Claus Westermann, *Genesis 12–36: A Commentary,* trans. John J. Scullion (Minneapolis: Augsburg, 1985), 164.

31. Niditch, "Genesis," 18–19.

32. Nahum M. Sarna, *The JPS Torah Commentary: Genesis* (Philadelphia: Jewish Publication Society, 1989), 94.

33. Niditch, "Genesis," 18. Wenham notes that in verse 15, "was taken" is an expression that "properly denotes the formal taking of a woman as a wife . . . it can be used more loosely to describe all aspects of marriage" (*Genesis 1–15,* 289).

34. Sarna, *The JPS Torah Commentary,* 94–95.

35. Thus, for example, Wenham reports the suggestion by E. A. Speiser that we find in this story "an allusion to a Hurrian custom whereby a man could take a

woman to be both wife and sister at the same time," and Wenham likewise observes that Speiser's hypothesis "is rejected by more recent writers" (Wenham, *Genesis 1–15*, 288; also see Westermann, *Genesis 12–36*, 164).

36. Gloria Anzaldúa, *Borderlands/La Frontera: The New Mestiza*, 2nd ed. (San Francisco: Aunt Lute Books, 1999), 34–35.

37. See Joseph Nevins, *Operation Gatekeeper: The Rise of the "Illegal Alien" and the Making of the U.S.-Mexico Boundary* (New York: Routledge, 2002).

38. United States Government Accountability Office, *Illegal Immigration: Border-Crossing Deaths Have Doubled Since 1995; Border Patrol's Efforts to Prevent Deaths Have Not Been Fully Evaluated* (Washington, DC: United States Government Accountability Office, 2006), 3, 13.

39. R. S. Sugirtharajah, "A Postcolonial Exploration," 113.

2

AKKAMAHADEVI AND THE SAMARITAN WOMAN

Paradigms of Resistance and Spirituality

Monica Jyotsna Melanchthon

Theological discourse and biblical interpretation in India today are being influenced by the postcolonial approach. Professor R. S. Sugirtharajah, in whose honor we dedicate this volume, is renowned for his contributions in this area, and his works have played a major role in inspiring and equipping our students with the tools and methods of this approach. It is with great pleasure that I dedicate this article to Prof. R. S. Sugirtharajah.

In the Indian context the collaboration of gender, caste, class, ethnicity, and the state complicate the task of theologizing and the expression of faith by any single religious community. It is obvious that we cannot theologize in isolation and that we need to step out of our own confessional frame of reference and draw from the wealth of multicultural and religious traditions. At the same time we need to work toward reclamation of images and find in them the fragility of protest and hope in the fragmented images and life stories.[1] This need for a relationship between our faith and other cultural patterns, both religious and secular, in order to articulate a theology and faith that is Indian, meaningful, and transformative has been stressed for some time by various theologians. Stanley J. Samartha emphasized the fact that there are many movements fighting for the rights of the marginalized and the discriminated. They are "secular" in the sense of being not obviously religious. They are not seeking scriptural hermeneutics or a religious theology of liberation before actually fighting for liberation. They may be religious individually but they do not flaunt their religious labels openly.[2]

In a multireligious society where people of different religious persuasions come together for a common human purpose in society, religious labels should not become hindrances. For example, for Christian women to experience emancipation, it is not sufficient that we liberate the Christian scriptures from their patriarchal moorings, but that we work with our sisters of other religious persuasions and together discover traditions within our cultures that might help us all in our struggle against discrimination and violence. Acts of protests and liberative streams are found even among other religious traditions and communities, which might in fact sensitize the hermeneutical antennae of biblical interpreters to discover fresh insights for bringing about God's liberation of both men and women in the totality of a reconciled humanity.

Behind the proposals of multifaith or multicultural hermeneutics lies this basic notion that by reading together and in relation to one another we might discover traditions that transcend structures of oppression derived from diverse sources outside of our own. This involves reading in juxtaposition. This essay seeks to study the life and some of the hagiographical poems or *vachanas* of Akkamahadevi of the *virasaiva* movement in twelfth-century India alongside that of the Samaritan woman (John 4). These texts will be looked at intertextually[3] in that I shall attempt to dialogue with these two texts using my personal experience as the third text. I hope that it will also be "contrapuntal" in that I will restrain from making any "authoritative claim for one religious tradition or the attribution of exclusive meaning to one text."[4] This attempt seeks to uncover possible similarities and differences, as well as shared insights that might contribute to our effort to reclaim images and traditions of protest and hope that transcend systems of subjugation and build alternative structures that contribute to the dignity and subjecthood of women and men.[5]

Akkamahadevi

The *bhakti* movement, which began in the south of India, eventually moving in continuing waves across regions, is known to have played a decisive role in shaping the social, cultural, and religious life of people of all religions in the subcontinent.[6] It enriched and synthesized traditions. An example of this synthesizing is seen in the interaction of *bhakti* and *Sufism* in north India. The liberating aspects of *bhakti* are well known.[7] The *bhaktas* asserted the equality of all people before God, regardless of caste and status, some even stressing that high status and wealth were hurdles to finding oneness with God. They emphasized love as being far more important than knowledge gained from book learning. Self-realization was seen as accessible even to the lowliest. The pride and self-righteousness of the religious and other authority figures was condemned.[8]

Through the introduction of the use of *bhakti marga*,[9] purity of soul and action and the shift from Sanskrit to vernacular languages in worship, the entry of women into the field of Hindu religion was made easier. During the twelfth century, with the birth of Virasaivism,[10] we note the entry of women into the sect not as mere passive followers but as religious leaders and saints.[11] By emphasizing that God dwelt in all — high and low alike — and by rejecting the intellectual approach (through books) as a way of reaching God, the *bhakti* movements opened their doors not just to supposedly low status groups but also to women. These women did not address themselves specifically to women. But with the rejection of the Brahmin's mediatory and superior role in rituals, women were now able to have direct access to God; they could also pray and worship at their convenience, even when nursing or being sick or poor. The freedom to use vernacular languages in worship and writing enabled these women to pen their own devotional lyrics and poems, thus making a contribution to modern Indian languages. The impediments created by a husband or in-laws often took a violent turn in the form of physical abuse, and in some instances ended up being fatal. Consequently, most women *bhakta* poets could proceed on their chosen path only by discarding their marital life, status, and wealth. Some refused marriage and others walked out of oppressive marriages. In addition, some of these women dramatically renounced the tyranny imposed by crippling notions of respectable feminine behavior. Most of them renounced not only marriage but also material wealth and status and chose the life of mendicants.

The specific social dimensions of the lives and work of the women *bhaktas*, by and large, have been neglected by scholarship. These extraordinarily courageous and creative women who asserted their right to their own life as they defined it have left a powerful social and cultural legacy for us. This legacy constitutes a living tradition even today, not only in the sense that their songs are an integral part of popular culture in their regions, but also because they are remembered and revered for having stood by their convictions in defiance of prevalent social norms. The work of these women and the legends surrounding each of them testify not only to their creativity but also to their joyous exploration of truth, even when this involved a radical departure from the life legislated for most women. Though the memory of them preserved in legends identifies them as symbols of pure selfless love, they are also renowned for poems of deep wisdom and philosophical thought. The vigor and sheer audacity with which they expressed their thoughts still have the capacity to move, inspire, and surprise us.

The more capable of the women who entered the sect provided leadership to the entire sect. In the *vachanas*[12] of Akkamahadevi, we find substantiation of this statement. She questions, "Do breasts alone make a person a female, and a moustache, a male?" She further declares, "I am woman in name and male in spirit."[13] "If a woman is a temptation to man, so is man to woman. . . . Temptation is thus in the mind of a person and not in the sex of a person."[14] The historian P. B. Desai describes Akkamahadevi "as a lady of exceptional philosophical heights."[15]

Akkamahadevi was born in Udutadi, a village near Shimoga in present-day Karnataka, and initiated into Virasaivism when still a young girl. The most popular legends about Akka, literally meaning "older sister," claim that Kausika, the king of that land, saw her one day and desired to have her as his wife. Kausika was a Jain, and it is important to remember that in Karnataka the Virasaiva movement was focused as much against this dominant commercial community as it was against the religious orthodoxy of the Brahmins. Akka would have consented to marry Kausika, but the claims of Shiva were stronger. A couple of her powerful poems, or *vachanas,* dramatize this tension between unqualified devotion to God and the expected single-minded service to the husband.

> *Husband inside,*
> *Lover outside.*
> *I can't manage them both.*

> *This world*
> *and that other*
> *cannot manage them both.*[16]

The second poem reads:

> *I love the Handsome One:*
> *he has no death*
> *decay nor form*
> *no place or side*
> *no end nor birthmarks*
> *I love him, O mother. Listen.*
> *I love the beautiful One*
> *with no bond nor fear*
> *no clan, no land*
> *no landmarks*
> *for his beauty.*
> > *So my Lord, white as jasmine, is*
> > *my husband.*
> *Take these husbands who die,*
> > *decay and feed them*
> > *to your kitchen fires!*[17]

Akkamahadevi warned her husband not to touch her against her will. In doing so, she actually challenged the laws of Manu that give the husband complete proprietary rights.[18] A respectable woman was not allowed to live by herself or outdoors or refuse sex to her husband.[19] Legend has it that Akka threatened to leave if Kausika ever touched her against her will. He did and she left. She wandered and traveled alone. She rejected the human lover, who would have turned her body into an object of his desire, in favor of her Chennamallikarjuna,[20] who gave form to her Self. She severed her ties with her mother and her birthplace and set out in search of her Lord Chennamallikarjuna, to whom she betrothed herself.[21]

> *I have Maya for mother-in-law,*
> *the world for father-in-law;*
> *three brothers-in-law, like tigers;*
> *and the husband's thoughts*
> *are full of laughing women;*

no god, this man.
And I cannot cross the sister-in-law.
But I will
Give this wench the slip
And go cuckold my husband with
Hara, my Lord.
My mind is my maid;
by her kindness, I join
   my Lord,
   my utterly beautiful Lord
   from the mountain-peaks,
   my Lord white as jasmine,
and I will make Him
my good husband.[22]

Her departure from the confines of domesticity gave her freedom to search for her god and lover. Even the pangs of hunger and thirst did not affect her since she has found her Lord.

For hunger,
   there is the town's rice in the
   begging bowl.
For thirst,
   there are tanks, streams, wells.
For sleep,
   there are the ruins of temples.
For soul's company
   I have you, O Lord,
white as jasmine.[23]

The manner in which she handled her marriage is in some ways linked to the deeper question of her sexuality and her explicit attitude to the female body. She wandered, some legends say, naked, covered only by the tresses of her hair,[24] across most of what is now Karnataka in search of her divine lover.

For Akka, her body and her sexuality were not embarrassing or impediments. The body was the instrument, the site through which her devotion found expression. Her relationship with the Lord was set within the framework of bridal mysticism.[25] Akka did not deny the female body.

She embraced it with a directness that is without parallel. But in embracing it the way she did, she forced the world around to do the same. Her brutal frankness saw no shame in stripping off conventional notions of modesty.[26] She has some wonderful verses on nakedness and modesty.

> *You can confiscate money in hand;*
> *Can you confiscate the body's glory?*
> *Or peel away every strip you wear?*
> *Can you peel the Nothing, the Nakedness*
> *that covers and veils?*
> *To the shameless girl*
> *wearing the white Jasmine Lord's*
> *light of morning,*
> *you fool,*
> *where's the need for cover and jewel?*[27]

She also writes:

> *People*
> *male and female,*
> *blush when a cloth covering their shame*
> *comes loose.*
> *When the Lord of lives*
> *lives drowned without a face*
> *in the world, how can you be modest?*
> *When all the world is the eye of the Lord,*
> *onlooking everywhere, what can you*
> *cover and conceal?*[28]

Throwing away clothes is a throwing away of concessions to social conventions, defenses, and investments. Nakedness signifies being open to the experiences of God.[29] Chakravarty writes,

As someone who has not denied her sexuality but at the same time seeks the liberation that other *bhaktas* have, she adopts a radical measure, and wanders about naked. . . . In a sense she flaunts her sexuality and defies an onslaught upon it. Her decision to strip off all clothing is a refusal to be circumscribed by the notion of the vulnerability of the female body, a refusal to make compromises because of it. In that sense she conquers the threat it poses and is the only *bhaktin* to do so.[30]

Akkamahadevi therefore refused to allow the female body to be an impediment in the search for salvation. She figured that violation in the outside world was no different from violation within the home.

Akka expresses her intense devotion and love for Shiva using the metaphor of illicit love, whom she addresses as "Chennamallikarjuna."

It is a relationship she seeks out, one she is intoxicated by and willingly abandons herself to, with a directness of address surprising even today. The three conventional poetic themes of love forbidden, love fulfilled, and the longing of separated lovers are often compressed into the same *vacana* and sometimes into one dominant image. The growth of carnal love becomes a symbol of mystic progression.[31]

Akka's poems are poignant and memorable. For the conventional woman and man, her work embodies a radical illegitimacy as she struggles in her poetry and lifestyle to go beyond societal expectations to include the struggles of her body, struggles against the pettiness of roles she is forced into as a woman, struggles against a man who is also a prince and a Jain, and against the social expectations that restrain her.

Akka saw God as male but in an idealized version of the conventional relationship of woman to man. The object of devotion was not a distant authoritative god but a companion. In such a model, there is an alternative for gender relationship. Through her *bhakti*, Akka was able to break through the Brahmanical social order and her circumscribed role within the home. She used her devotion as an armor and God as her supporter in her resistance against the priest and the husband.

The Samaritan Woman[32]

On a literary level, the evangelist John's stories of the Samaritans (Jn 4:4–42) and the royal official (Jn 4:46–54) conclude a sequence of stories which, beginning with 2:1, deal with the way individuals have responded to Jesus. John 4:1–42 narrates Jesus' encounter with a Samaritan[33] woman as he rested by Jacob's well in Sychar in Samaria while his disciples were in the city buying food. The Samaritan woman's eventual response to Jesus is contrasted with that of the Pharisees (4:1–3). The dialogue between Jesus and the anonymous Samaritan woman concludes with her recognizing Jesus as the Messiah and the Samaritan community proclaiming Jesus as the "savior of the world." The story has therefore been included to account for the Samaritan acceptance of a Jewish Messiah and Savior and the inclusion of a Samaritan component within the Christian community familiar to the gospel writer.[34] The story also stresses the reconciliation and healing of the fractured relationship between the Jews and the Samaritans.[35] I do not intend to address the many questions the passage raises with regard to the identity of the Samaritans, the cause of the rift between the Jews and the Samaritans, the historicity of Jesus' ministry in Samaria,[36] the location of Sychar,[37] the symbolism of the living water,[38] or whether the passage intends to present Jesus as the only savior of the world.[39] For these have been done by a host of commentators. My focus in this section will be the person and character of the Samaritan woman and what we learn from her as an individual.

It was noon and Jesus, tired from his journey to Galilee from Judea, rested at the well of Jacob while his disciples went off into the city to buy food. A woman came by to draw water and she belonged to a community that, in the parlance of present-day Indian society, could be considered a *Dalit* community. The Samaritans were marginalized because of their place of origin and were considered inferior by the Jews.[40] They were also marginalized because they were considered to be ignorant of the Torah, ritually impure, and outside the boundaries of God's people. The location of this encounter between Jesus and the Samaritan woman is also significant in that water and wells are contested things in the Indian context. There are still areas in India where *Dalits* are not allowed to draw water from the village wells owned by the dominant caste just as they are not allowed entry into some temples. Women have to go a distance to bring water. "Therefore, water, the primeval women's issue, which is also a crucial *Dalit* issue, becomes the focus of her conversation with Jesus."[41] But the location of this encounter is also significant because it accentuates two things: first, the common human need for water that draws both characters to the well, which then becomes the meeting point of two cultures, two communities, and two religions. Second, the well is one that belonged to Jacob, and hence it serves to underscore the common ancestry of Jesus and the Samaritan woman, two individuals who are now divided due to historical and social circumstances.

It is midday, which is the meeting point of the two halves of the day, and not the usual time when women go to bring water. Women are known to go in pairs or in groups to bring water, but most commentators understand that this woman is alone. Many commentators identify her as a "sinful woman"[42] on the basis of verses 16 through 18, which report that she had been married five times and was now living with a man who was not her husband. She has been isolated and shunned, according to commentators, and now draws water by herself because of this. Avoided as a woman of ill repute, she was disrespected because she did not conform to social norms. According to biblical scholar Gerard Sloyan, she is oppressed threefold for "she is a woman, a Samaritan and a polygamist."[43] We shall return to verses 16 through 18 later.

I wonder how appropriate it is to assume that she was an isolated woman. The text does not mention that she was alone, nor does it state or give the impression that there were others beside her at the well. I contest readings that claim she was alone. It is possible that there might have been others, but that Jesus chose her to enter into a conversation.[44] Even if she had come alone, could she not have done so because she ran out of water at home, even after having brought some early that morning? Maybe she could not come in the morning, and this was the first opportunity she had to come to the well. There is no specific time for drawing water, is there? Her coming alone need not therefore be an indication of her isolation or rejection, considering the fact that she was later instrumental in bringing members of her community to Jesus. Who would pay attention to her if she was as immoral as she has been made out to be?

Against known conventions, Jesus, a Jew, asks the woman for a drink. The woman, aware of the historical and political background of the enmity between the two communities, expresses surprise at Jesus' request for water from her. The narrator's side remark that "Jews do not share things in common with Samarians" reveals another aspect of the conflict between the two communities. The Jews did not eat or drink from the same vessels as the Samaritans for fear of defiling their purity.[45] Her reluctance to give water is not because she was prejudiced against the Jews as maintained by Mlakuzhyil,[46] but because she was aware of the consequences of her action. She may have internalized the notion that she was impure and that she would be polluting this Jew if he drank water that she drew from the well. Even if she served water at the behest of Jesus, it is she as the unclean one, the outcast, the Samaritan who would be blamed and found at fault. Her response was one of concern that her action might have social implications for both parties.[47] I think that her concern was more for Jesus than herself.[48]

Jesus' response prompts further questions from the woman that reveal the extent of her knowledge. That the woman was aware of the political and social conflict between the Jews and the Samaritans is obvious, but she was also a woman who was theologically astute. She had many questions, indicating that she was vocal and unafraid to ask questions of this stranger. She is argumentative and shows courage. Her questions also reveal her knowledge regarding her faith. It is she who calls attention to the original owner of the well, "Jacob our father," and hence makes a veiled attempt to stress their common ancestry. But the subject turns from the physical need for water to thirst in a spiritual sense, which will be quenched once and for all. She was clearly not happy with having to come to the well for water because of the inconvenience of the distance and the labor involved. She was eager for some of that "living water" that she was told would not make her thirsty again. She had understood the "living water"[49] only in a literal sense. Then Jesus requests her to come back with her husband.

The response of Jesus to the woman's request is not only surprising but also odd. Why does Jesus ask her to bring her husband? Does Jesus want to convert both at the same time? Some scholars have read this instruction as due to Jesus' "supernatural knowledge" and that it was meant "to lead her into a confession" for her "corrupt practices."[50] It is a request, according to Mlakuzhyil, which serves as a "gentle prod" to "help her see if there is any block that would prevent the flow of 'living water' into her heart."[51]

The Samaritan woman's five husbands have been the topic of much discussion among scholars as the reason for her being labeled a "sinful woman." Some scholars seem to be uncomfortable with this possibility. They doubt the literal truth of this information and hence prefer to understand the five husbands allegorically as the five books of Moses that were authoritative for the Samaritans, or as the gods worshipped by the Samaritans,[52] or the five idolatrous people of the East identified in 2 Kings 17:24, 30–31, with the sixth being the worship on Mount Gerizim considered idolatrous by the Jews.[53] If this were the case, who

is it that Jesus instructed the woman to bring? And how does one understand the woman's answer, "I have no husband"? It seems to me that
these male scholars are disturbed by the notion of a woman with multiple
partners, and hence question its historical probability.[54] My guess is also
that something is probably lost here, some further dialog between Jesus
and the Samaritan woman that led to this instruction, "Go call your
husband."[55] Even if these "five husbands" were to be understood allegorically or symbolically, the use of this literary device has several
implications. If polyandry was not common, why was it alluded to here?
A Samaritan man with five wives could have served the same purpose.
Is it because a woman with multiple partners is far more effective as a
symbol of "sinfulness and impurity" than a man?

I would press for a more literal reading of this text. The woman is an
individual but also representative of the collective, an oppressed group. I
offer here an interpretation by a group of women students at the Gurukul
Lutheran Theological College on the occasion of International Women's
Day in 2004. The women enacted the narrative of the Samaritan woman,
portraying the woman protagonist as an outcast *Dalit* woman who meets
Jesus at the well designated for *Dalits* and engages Jesus in a conversation about caste and culture in India. The woman is shown as being
responsible for introducing Jesus to a day in the life of a *Dalit* woman,
which includes domestic work such as fetching water and firewood, work
in the fields of the dominant caste landowner, and sexual harassment,
often violent, by both *Dalit* and non-*Dalit* men. And yet amid all this,
the woman would make time at the end of the day to hold the Bible,
which she could not read on account of illiteracy, and pray.

The woman then narrates her story of how she ended up having five
husbands. She explains and each of her explanations is enacted as a
scene. First she tells Jesus that she is not allowed by both law and the
culture to divorce her husband. However, her first husband divorced her
on account of her bringing an insufficient dowry. Another came forward
to marry her, but divorced her since she was unable to bear a male child.
The third man who married her was an alcoholic who beat her black
and blue every night, and she ran away unable to tolerate the violence.
The fourth man was much older than she was and was poor and sickly.
He died. The fifth husband divorced her for a younger woman.

But Jesus, hearing the story, makes no moral judgment or condemnation. Contrary to the acknowledged norm, Jesus offers forgiveness. The

woman's plight is simply acknowledged as a fact of life that in no way denigrates her. Jesus offers her "living water," the capacity for physical emancipation from the drudgery and pain of caste labor, violence, discrimination, and suffering. "Living water" is understood as the empowerment that comes by being equipped with the mechanisms and the mind set to resist and overcome caste. It is this *Dalit* consciousness that energizes the woman and motivates her to share this good news with her community, and in turn to mobilize them to defy caste and its many concomitant results. The woman begins with the recognition that Jesus is a Jew. Then, as the dialog with Jesus continues and as he leads her forward by his responses, she sees him as someone perhaps greater than Jacob, then as a prophet and as the Messiah.[56] Indeed, she gradually becomes so convinced of his exalted identity that she eventually proclaims him to her townspeople. The woman was instrumental in the extension of the Jesus movement to the Samaritan community.[57] By allowing her to be his spokesperson, Jesus transcends the confines of community and religion. Jesus foretells a time when neither Jerusalem nor Gerizim will be a place of worship. Rather, God can be worshiped anywhere in spirit and in truth.[58] In the words of theologian Gabriele Dietrich, "By this he [Jesus] denies all communal claims to a specific place and he also implicitly rejects the zealotic option of anti-colonial uprising for the liberation of the temple. With this, the initial controversy about the holy mountain (v. 20ff) becomes obsolete."[59]

The Samaritan community is first impressed and persuaded by the testimony of the woman, which creates openness to Jesus. She expresses her doubt as to whether he was the Messiah, further adding to the curiosity of the people and giving them a reason to seek him out. They come to Jesus and invite Jesus to "remain" with them for a while, and Jesus accepts. Many from the village come to believe in him and are conscientized. Finally, the Samaritans make a culminating confession that Jesus is "savior of the world."[60] The students did not address the identity of the sixth man in the woman's life. I would like to propose that the woman, after having had multiple experiences of marriage that ended in pain, intentionally avoided marriage and chose a companion to live with, without the encumbrances that come with marriage.[61] This companion had no authority over her. He was her mate and partner. I think she was an attractive woman physically, which made her desirable for men who were in favor of overlooking the fact that she was married before. If the woman agreed to marry again, it was probably driven by a sense of insecurity and an existential need since life for a widow was hard.[62] It seems that the Samaritans were far more tolerant about this than the Jews.

Women are not passive recipients of welfare, but in fact could become active promoters and facilitators of social transformations. Such transformations influence the lives and well-being not only of women but also of men and children. The Samaritan woman, after having had a few hard experiences, realized that she needed to come into her own. She defied accepted social norms and customs. She was able to transcend barriers of gender and religion and made a space for herself that was characterized by freedom and agency. She was courageous and willing to face the odds. This was her way of protesting against the societal norms and expectations. Because she was not tied to a man, she was able to speak to Jesus, alone or otherwise, and share the benefits of her conversation with the rest of the community. And for this, she is remembered and celebrated.

Conclusion

Gabriele Dietrich calls attention to the similarity in the structure of protest and transcendence in the two women characters discussed above.[63] It is significant that both Akkamahadevi and the Samaritan woman who defied convention in many startling ways were not persecuted or dismissed but respected in their lifetimes. They became part of living and growing traditions. The sexuality and eroticism of Akkamahadevi and the multiple partners/husbands of the Samaritan woman are probably uncomfortable for many of us. But what needs to be acknowledged is that we continue to read their stories that have been preserved. This in itself is evidence of a very positive aspect of both traditions — their capacity to make social space available for women with exceptionally outstanding abilities. They exhibit courage even when they have outrageously defied what are ordinarily considered the fundamental tenets of *stree dharma,* marriage, and motherhood.[64] These women contributed to building a culture wherein women who devote themselves to the pursuit of some goal higher than self-interest, and who demonstrate an ability to stay steadfast to their chosen ideals, are not made objects of derision, but are given special respect, even homage. This is true even when they choose to opt out of marriage in an otherwise marriage-obsessed culture.[65] One contemporary argument often put forward against recognition of such women is that since they operated within a religious framework and used a religious idiom, they can function only as useful symbols for activists. This criticism ignores the fact that much of the history of protest across the world has been couched in a religious idiom. Besides, religious protest always has had social as well as religious dimensions.

In terms of lived actuality, the chosen god of a woman devotee or disciple, whether or not posited as husband or lover, was not the simple equivalent of a male authority figure for the simple and good reason that the god was not physically present to dictate or obstruct as the father or husband. The woman's god, whether dwelling within or in an image to which she ascribes attributes, justifies her actions even though they may seem unjustifiable to others. Thus with "god's help," the woman *bhakta* or disciple negotiates that social space which is not available to other women. She finds a new community and sets out on her quest. God's voice is the decisive voice a woman can cite as a legitimate authority for rejecting societal and familial authority. In the case of the Samaritan woman, she chose a companion who would probably have no authority over her. Being unmarried, she too was able to create for herself a social space not available to married women. Both women found some security in these relationships. Akkamahadevi does not receive God's orders from any external authority except a guru she may have chosen. The interpretation of what God requires is essentially made by her. She decides to discard clothing, her husband, her marriage, and slavery to family honor. All of this is legitimized only because she does so for God. The religious path was perhaps the only legitimate path available to her and other women *bhaktas* as an escape from the narrow confines of domesticity.

The *bhakta*'s poetry is not protest literature as the term is understood today. Both women do not carry, I believe, an easily decipherable social message for other women. Most of it is a celebration of individual choice. Nor do they call for an overall gender equality. To say this is not to view them as somehow inadequate. The idea of gender equality as a desirable and obtainable social and political ideal is a relatively new idea in human history. To look for its expression in contemporary terms by these women would be to do an injustice to both the past and the present. In order to move our society in the direction of greater justice

and freedom we need to develop a creative relationship with the more humane and potentially liberating aspects of our cultural traditions. These
women represent illegitimate, subversive, or transgressing relationships.
These women, though victims of atrocity, attain new power by renewed
transgression. Their sovereignty is expressed in the extra-ordinariness of
their family situation.[66]

Notes

1. Gabriele Dietrich, "On Doing Feminist Theology in Asia," in *A New Thing
on Earth: Hopes and Fears Facing Feminist Theology,* ed. Gabriele Dietrich (New
Delhi: ISPCK, 2001), 104.

2. Stanley J. Samartha, " 'But if it is a daughter she shall live': Feminist Hermeneutics in Asian Christian Theology" in *Theology of Humanhood: Women's
Perspectives,* ed. Aruna Gnanadason (New Delhi: ISPCK, 1986), 106.

3. Jean Delorme, "Intertextualities about Mark," in *Intertextuality in Biblical
Writings: Essays in Honor of Bas van Iersel,* ed. Spike Draisma (Kampen: J. H.
Kok, 1989), 35; see also A. Maria Arulraja, "Breaking Hegemonic Boundaries: An
Intertextual Reading of the Madurai Veeran Legend and Mark's Story of Jesus," in
Voices from the Margin: Interpreting the Bible in the Third World, rev. and expanded
3rd ed., ed. R. S. Sugirtharajah (Maryknoll, NY: Orbis Books, 2006), 103–4.

4. R. S. Sugirtharajah, "Postcolonial Criticism and Asian Biblical Studies," in
*Critical Engagement in the Asian Context: Implications for Theological Education
and Christian Studies,* ed. Preman Niles (Hong Kong: Asian Christian Higher Education Institute, 2005), 78; see also R. S. Sugirtharajah, "A Postcolonial Exploration
of Collusion and Construction in Biblical Interpretation," in *The Postcolonial Bible,*
ed. R. S. Sugirtharajah (Sheffield: Sheffield Academic Press, 1998), 94; *Asian Biblical Hermeneutics and Postcolonialism: Contesting Interpretations* (Maryknoll, NY:
Orbis Books, 1998), 116ff.

5. Jione Havea, *Elusions of Control: Biblical Law on the Words of Women*
(Boston and Leiden: Brill, 2003), 4, uses "transtextuality," which allows for a similar
crossing of these texts but with an intentional privileging of the non-biblical text.
I do not begin with the privileging of any text but with the final interpretation or
meaning that is arrived at by the process of evaluation and analysis that might lead
me to favor one over against the other in the light of its relevance and import on the
reader or myself.

6. Scholarly consensus today tends to view *bhakti* as a post-Vedic development
that took place primarily in the watershed years of the epics and *puranas*, litera-
tures that are credited with a primary role in the cultural transition from *vedism* to
Hinduism. *Bhakti* in India is preeminently a monotheistic reform movement. The
inextricable connections between monotheism and reform had both theological and
social significance in terms of the development of Indian culture; see Karen Pechillis
Prentiss, *The Embodiment of Bhakti* (New York: Oxford University, 1999), 13–17.

7. A unitary approach to *bhakti* is not viable. There are ideological differences
in the position adopted by the medieval *bhaktas*. Besides religious modes, organiza-
tional aspects of the sects, the origins of which are attributed to this movement, show

a wide range of variations. Hence it is not a unified or homogenous movement as such. The designation covers a number of movements, each with its own distinctive features and ethos. Some of them were even antithetical to one another, notwithstanding their common commitment to *bhakti*. The *bhakti* movement is therefore a multiplex phenomenon and the nature of its impact also had many dimensions. See Krishna Sharma, *Bhakti and the Bhakti Movement. A New Perspective: A Study in the History of Ideas* (New Delhi: Munshiram Manoharlal, 1987), 1.

8. Madhu Kishwar, "Introduction," *Manushi*, 10th anniversary issue, nos. 50, 51, 52 (1989): 4.

9. Intense personal love, devotion, and dedication to God.

10. The Lingayats or Virasaivas comprised a sect founded by Basavva, a minister of King Bijjala Kalacuri, who usurped the throne of the Chalukyas of Kalyani in 1156 C.E. This sect is noteworthy for its cult and social doctrines rather than for its theology, which is a qualified monism. Basavva opposed image worship. Only the sacred symbol of the *linga* of Shiva was carried by his followers. He rejected the Vedas and the authority of the Brahman class, and ordained a new priesthood called the *jaògamas*. He opposed pilgrimage and sacrifice, condemned cremation, and instituted complete equality among his followers, even to the equality of women, who were permitted to remarry on the death of their husband. See A. L. Bashan, *The Wonder That Was India*, 3rd rev. ed. (New Delhi: Rupa, 1967), 335.

11. The term "saint" is rarely associated with miracle makers as is done in Christianity. It is deeply associated with persons of virtue and religiosity.

12. Poetry.

13. Nandimath Menezes et al., eds., *Surya Sampadane* 2 (1868–72), chap. 16, 44.

14. Source not mentioned. As cited by Leela Mullatti, *The Bhakti Movement and the Status of Women: A Case Study of Virasaivism* (New Delhi: Abhinav Publications, 1989), 7.

15. P. B. Desai, *Basaveswara and His Time* (Dharwar: Karnatak University, 1968), 18. In India, religion engulfs major portions of one's life — so both entry and active contribution in the religious field by women is a clear indication of their improvement in status.

16. A. K. Ramanujan, *Speaking of Siva* (London: Penguin, 1973), 127.

17. Ibid., 134.

18. Manu leaves nothing un-codified as far as women are concerned. Marriage is indissoluble, divorce impossible, and widow remarriage never permitted for "respectable women." Chapter 5:165 of the *Manusmriti* says, "She who, controlling her thoughts, words, and deeds, never slights her lord, resides (after death) with her husband (in heaven), and is called a virtuous (wife)" (trans. G. Buhler; available on the Internet at *www.hinduism.about.com/library/weekly/extra/bl-lawsofmanu1.htm* [accessed on April 25, 2007]). See also chapter 5:147ff of the Laws of Manu for further injunctions about women that emphasize their complete subjugation to men.

19. "She must not seek to separate herself from her father, husband, or sons; by leaving them she would make both (her own and her husband's) families contemptible" (*Manusmriti*, chap. 5, 149).

20. Translated as "Lord, white as jasmine." Literally it would be rendered "Mallika's Arjuna." See Susie Tharu and K. Lalitha, *Women Writing in India: 600 B.C. to the Present, volume 1: 600 B.C. to the Early 20th Century* (New Delhi: Oxford University, 1993), 77.

21. Tharu and Lalitha, *Women Writing in India*, 77.

22. Ramanujan, *Speaking of Siva*, 141.

23. Ibid., 132.

24. Available at *www.poetseers.org/the_great_poets/female_poets/spiritual_and _devotional_poets/india/mah*; see also *www.poetry-chaikhana.com* for an image of Akkamahadevi.

25. Tharu and Lalitha, *Women Writing in India*, 77.

26. R. G. Mathapati writes, "However, she, defending her disregard for body and clothes, says I have killed the cupid in myself and conquered this world. So I have no body. When I have no body, no sex, where does exist the question of clothes?" (available at *www.ourkarnataka.com/religion/akka_mathapati*).

27. Ramanujan, *Speaking of Siva*, 129.

28. Ibid., 184.

29. "When women throw away clothes, they are also throwing away the attractive parts of womanhood that are sexual come-ons of which modesty is one. Women saints did have to contend with the problem of sexual advances from the males around them. Modesty, like clothes, is a way of resisting and enhancing sexual curiosity, not of curbing it. It is this paradox that is exposed when clothes are thrown away" (A. K. Ramanujan, "Talking to God in the Mother Tongue," in *Manushi*, 10th anniversary issue, nos. 50, 51, 52 (1989): 13.

30. Uma Chakravarty, "The World of the Bhaktin in South Indian Traditions — the Body and Beyond," in *Manushi*, 10th anniversary issue, nos. 50, 51, 52 (1989): 27.

31. Tharu and Lalitha, *Women Writing in India*, 77.

32. See *www.asianchristianart.org/galleries/samaritanwoman* for artwork on the Samaritan woman by Asians.

33. "Samaritan" (Greek *Samaritēs*) was originally a geographic term, an inhabitant of Samaria (Hebrew *šomeron*), the capital of the northern kingdom, founded by Omri, ca. 870 B.C.E. In time it became an ethnic and religious name for the inhabitants of the area between Judea and Galilee, west of the Jordan. The origin of the split of the Samaritans from the Jews is shrouded in mystery and explained differently in each group. . . . In any case, these (half-Jewish?) worshippers of Yahweh . . . built a temple on part of Mount Gerizim (Tell-er-Ras) in Hellenistic times. . . . From Hellenistic times on the sharp division of Jews and Samaritans is clear; the Samartians developed their own form of the Pentateuch (redacted in Hasmonean times), their own liturgy" (Joseph A. Fitzmyer, *The Gospel according to Luke*, Anchor Bible 28–28A [Garden City, NY: Doubleday, 1981], 829).

34. Gerard S. Sloyan, *John*, Interpretation (Atlanta: John Knox, 1988), 52; Robert J. Karris, O.F.M., *Jesus and the Marginalized in John's Gospel* (Collegeville, MN: Liturgical Press, 1990), 70.

35. Sloyan, *John*, 56.

36. J. J. Kanagaraj, *The Gospel of John: A Commentary* (Secunderabad: OM Books, 2005), 140–41.

37. Ibid., 141–42.

38. George Mlakuzhyil, S.J., *Abundant Life in the Gospel of John* (New Delhi: Views/ISPCK, 2007), 69–71.

39. Richard J. Cassidy, *John's Gospel in New Perspective: Christology and the Realities of Roman Power* (Maryknoll, NY: Orbis Books, 1992), 35.

40. Karris, *Jesus and the Marginalized in John's Gospel*, 54–55.

41. Dietrich, "On Doing Feminist Theology in Asia," 106.

42. Mlakuzhyil, *Abundant Life in the Gospel of John*, 76; Kanagaraj, *The Gospel of John*, 146–47; Ben Witherington, III, *Women in the Ministry of Jesus: A Study of Jesus' Attitudes to Women and Their Roles as Reflected in His Earthly Life* (Cambridge: Cambridge University, 1984), 63.

43. The Samaritans did not observe all the regulations that the Jews did, and hence there was the suspicion that they, and especially the women of menstruating age, would be unclean. This uncleanness would be transmitted to the vessel the woman was carrying, especially if she had drunk from it. See Karris, *Jesus and the Marginalized in John's Gospel*, 69; Sloyan, *John*, 54.

44. Artists have also contributed to this interpretation by painting the woman as a lone figure by the well with Jesus. But see the painting of the Samaritan woman by Ven Hatigammana Uttarananda of Sri Lanka, who depicts several women at the well with one of them pouring water for Jesus to drink. Available at *www.asianchristianart.org/galleries/samaritanwoman*.

45. Kanagaraj, *The Gospel of John*, 142.

46. Mlakuzhyil, *Abundant Life in the Gospel of John*, 69.

47. I am reminded here of an incident narrated by a pastor from the south of India who, in the middle of a journey, knocked on the door of a house to ask for water. The woman heard his request and noticing that he was in his cassock concluded that he was a *Dalit* and shut the door in his face. If the Samaritan woman had been prejudiced, her response to Jesus' request may have been different.

48. The narrative bears similarities with a Buddhist parallel that narrates the encounter of Ananda, a disciple of Buddha, with a low-caste woman who refuses him water on account of her caste. See J. E. Bruns, *The Christian Buddhism of St. John: New Insights into the Fourth Gospel* (New York: Paulist Press, 1971), 24–59.

49. The question of eternal life that Jesus gives and promises is explained throughout the Gospel. "Water, wine, bread, light, truth, way, vine, door, word, are essential to human life because without them people perish" (Elisabeth Schüssler Fiorenza, *In Memory of Her: A Feminist Theological Reconstruction of Christian Origins* [London: SCM, 1983], 328). The gospel writer uses everyday realities and things to convey the divine or heavenly. These images both symbolize Jesus himself and at the same time, gifts for life, the living and life-giving divine powers that lead to eternal life.

50. Kanagaraj, *The Gospel of John*, 146–47.

51. Mlakuzhyil, *Abundant Life in the Gospel of John*, 71.

52. See Kanagaraj, *The Gospel of John*, 147.

53. Sloyan, *John*, 55.

54. I am also reminded here of Draupadi in the *Mahabharatha*, who marries the five Pandava brothers, proving that polyandry was known by other cultures as well.

55. I agree that this is just one possible way of trying to make sense of the passage. But I will still hold on to the notion that Jesus' words do not make any sense.

56. Schüssler Fiorenza, *In Memory of Her*, 138.

57. Ibid., 138.

58. "Spirit and in truth" is understood here as the mind-set of those who are made holy through their encounter with Jesus and who have transcended barriers of caste, religion, or community, those for whom "social-religious distinctions between Jews

and Samaritans, women and men no longer have any validity" (Schüssler Fiorenza, *In Memory of Her,* 138).

59. Dietrich, "On Doing Feminist Theology in Asia," 106.

60. Cassidy (*John's Gospel in New Perspective,* 35) claims that there are factors within this passage itself and within the larger framework of the Gospel to suggest the Samaritans' ringing acclamation belongs only to Jesus and not to any other person or entity.

61. Schottroff calls attention to the fact that it is normal for a woman to be identified in terms of her relationship to a man in biblical and extrabiblical materials. Contrary to patriarchal expectations, the New Testament presents many women as autonomous characters with no reference to any kinship relationship with father, brother, or husband. As a rule they are not to be regarded as unmarried or divorced. But judging by Schottorff's survey, it seems that autonomous women were more common than is normally accepted. The Samaritan woman is one who is neither named nor identified in relation to a male. See Luise Schottroff, Silvia Schroer, and Marie-Theres Wacker, *Feminist Interpretation: The Bible in Women's Perspective,* trans. Martin and Barbara Rumscheidt (Minneapolis: Fortress Press, 1998), 190–91.

62. In a recent Hindi movie entitled *Choker Bali,* the woman protagonist is a young widow in colonial India who is censured by the community because she was a young widow, literate, and educated by a white woman. She bemoans the fact that society recognizes all these but does not see her as a woman of flesh and blood with needs.

63. Dietrich, "On Doing Feminist Theology in Asia," 109.

64. Note the women mentioned in the genealogy of Jesus.

65. This is also evident from the easy acceptance of women in India as figures of authority in spheres normally considered male preserves. Just as the social acceptance of the women *bhaktas* did not result in expanding options for other ordinary women, so also the easy acceptance of outstanding women in unusual roles today does not indicate our society's willingness to grant ordinary women their basic human rights. This duality pervades all aspects of our social and cultural life. See Madhu Kishwar, "Of Humans and Divines," *Manushi,* 10th anniversary issue, nos. 50, 51, 52 (1989): 21.

66. Gabriele Dietrich, "Subversion, Transgression, Transcendence: 'Asian Spirituality' in the Light of Dalit and Adivasi Struggles," in *A New Thing on Earth: Hopes and Fears Facing Feminist Theology,* ed. Gabriele Dietrich (New Delhi: ISPCK, 2001), 246.

3

A TALE OF TWO CONVERSIONS

The Mighty Are Brought Down
and the Lowly Are Reluctant

CHARLES AMJAD-ALI

The story of the conversion of Cornelius in Acts 10 is inherently a story of multivalent cross-border communication: across Gentile and Jew, colonial and colonized, powerful and oppressed, the extreme center and the extreme periphery, and of absolute might and absolute vulnerability. Its hermeneutics, therefore, must reflect at least all these aspects. When read only from a classical "mainstream" perspective, it fails to reflect the robust vibrancy such a hermeneutics demands. For one must bear in mind the essentially colonial/imperial setting in which this story takes place in order to understand both the dynamics being portrayed here and the implications that this tale of two conversions has for world Christianity today.

The conversion of Cornelius is largely regarded as the beginning of the Gentile mission. It is not in fact the first exogenous conversion (or perhaps even the first Gentile conversion, depending on how one identifies the Ethiopian eunuch in 8:26–40). However, it is the conversion of Cornelius and his household that first invokes the consternation, controversy, and almost condemnation by the "circumcision" party against the direct conversion of the Gentiles without a Jewish mediation. The direct conversion of Gentiles is only grudgingly accepted in Acts 11 and is finally ecclesially resolved at the Jerusalem Council in Acts 15.[1]

At the beginning of Acts, during the first encounter with the disciples, the resurrected Jesus (1:3–9) promises them that "you will be my witnesses in Jerusalem, in all Judea and Samaria, and to the ends of the earth" (1:8). This is now being fulfilled here in the conversion of Cornelius. Post-Pentecost, the mission has already begun in Jerusalem and in all Judea and vast numbers of Jews are being converted throughout the region (2:41; 4:4; 5:14). The mission to the Samaritans has also taken place (8:5–25). Although the Samaritans were outside the orthodox Jewish community, the apostles in Jerusalem appear not to have any serious problem with their conversion as they did with Cornelius.[2]

The conversion of the Samaritans sets the tone for an increasingly expansive inclusion into the community of Jesus Christ. The next in this progression is that of the Ethiopian eunuch (8:27–28), whose religious status is unclear. Though he had come to Jerusalem to worship (8:27) and was reading the book of Isaiah as he traveled (8:28), both of which indicate his Jewishness, as a eunuch could he have been accepted to worship in Jerusalem? Even as one born into the Jewish faith this would have been very difficult (Dt 23:1); for a proselyte eunuch this must have been impossible. He shows a lack of knowledge of the scriptural interpretive traditions, but the passage he is reading just precedes one of the great inclusive passages in Isaiah that deals with foreigners, eunuchs, and outcasts (Is 56:1–8). By highlighting this conversion and not announcing his faith, Luke is perhaps making an eschatological claim for Christianity and its inclusion of all mentioned in Isaiah 56. What we do know, however, is that this is a significant conversion: Phillip is twice guided to the eunuch by the divine (8:26, 29), and the Holy Spirit carries him away after the Ethiopian has been baptized in water. It is important to note that in both the Samaritan and the Ethiopian cases, Phillip appears to have been baptized in water. Also, in the case of the Samaritans the baptism is in the name of the Lord Jesus (8:16), and in 2:38 it is in the name of Jesus Christ. Neither is in the name of the Trinity as demanded in Matthew 28:19.

The role of the Holy Spirit in these conversion narratives differentiates the conversions of the ambiguously exogenous Samaritans and the Ethiopian from that of the patently Gentile Cornelius and his household. Other differences of importance could be that the Samaritan conversions are generically described (except for the uncertain conversion of Simon, 8:5–25). We know quite a bit of detail about the Ethiopian but his name is never given. In the case of Cornelius, we not only have all the relevant details, even hyperbolized to make a point, but most important we have a name.

The Vision of Cornelius

It is surely not accidental that this story of the first Gentile conversion is set between Caesarea Maritima and Joppa. The former is utterly symbolic of the classical sycophancy of colonized leadership, for it was built and named after Augustus Caesar by Herod the Great to honor his colonial patron. Appropriately, after Herod's death it became the capital of the Roman province of Judea, the official seat of the Roman governor as well as a military base. Thus it was both the coercive and administrative center of Roman colonial power in the region. It is no wonder then that it is also the first site of the rebellion/revolt in 66 C.E. Joppa, on the other hand, is almost the binary opposite of Caesarea. It was under the direct control of the Jewish high priest after 46 B.C.E., but its importance was already minimal after the construction of Caesarea, and it was destroyed in 67 C.E. because it supported the Jewish Revolt.

The main protagonist in this tale is Cornelius: a centurion of the Italian cohort, and a man who fears God. Everything that Luke tells us about this man is redolent with meaning, even if that meaning is not always clear or unambiguous. To begin with, his name Cornelius is at this time almost exclusively associated with slavery and freed persons.[3] He is an officer in the Roman army, a symbol of Roman imperial power. It is interesting to note that the first colonial Gentile to have an encounter with Jesus (Lk 7:2–10; Mt 8:5–13) and the first Gentile to be converted to Christianity are both centurions. In other words, those who have coercively maintained the colonial hegemony are being converted to the religion of a double minority and the most vulnerable community in Judea at the time.

The fact that Cornelius is of the Italian cohort clearly implies that he is a Roman citizen.[4] What Luke is trying to say by imparting this seemingly trivial information (veracity and factuality notwithstanding) is that Cornelius is not a Syrian recruit picked up for a colonial task, but is actually from Italy, the seat of imperialist power. He is appointed for the Italian cohort and now stationed in the colonies. At stake is the true status of this man. He is more powerful in the hierarchy of the colonial power than those who serve from the colonies and even those who are appointed from Italy but exclusively for colonial positions.[5] This is critical for Luke, because through this hyperbole he can make a comparative display of the lowly status of Peter, a fisherman, who is residing at the home of a tanner, two "untouchables" in the Jewish social system. Thus Luke once again illustrates his theological assertion that "He [the Lord] has brought down the powerful from their thrones, and lifted up the lowly" of the *Magnificat* (1:46–55; especially v. 52). Western scholars tend to miss this because they are usually focusing on historical veracity rather than on the significant point that Luke is making about the character, power, and status of Cornelius and where he must seek his salvation.

Cornelius is described as devout and fearing God, along with his entire household. His credentials are that he gives alms generously to the people and prays constantly to God. The consensus of scholarship is that Cornelius is depicted as a Gentile who is attracted to Judaism, but is not a proselyte (i.e., following the Torah and circumcised but still of Gentile birth). Fitzmyer asserts that while *eusebēs* (devout) is generic, when put together with the "quasi-technical" phrase of "God-fearer," it denotes "non-Jewish sympathetic to Judaism, those who did not submit to circumcision or observe the Torah in its entirety, but who did agree with the ethical monotheism of the Jews and attended their synagogue services."[6] That Cornelius gave alms to the "Jewish people" is used as evidence to support this assertion. *Laos* (literally "people"), when used by Luke, is seen to mean the nation of Israel.[7] The language, however, does not seem to support this, especially here and later in 10:22, because it is not said that Cornelius gave charity specifically to the Jews, unlike the centurion in Luke 7:5, who "built our synagogue for us," a substantial financial contribution to the Jewish community. Yet even this latter example of religious generosity need not imply any specific affiliation with Judaism, since it is totally in line with the construction of the Second Temple, which was built almost completely through the support of Gentiles from Cyrus, through Darius, to Artaxerxes (see 2 Chr 36:22–23; Ezra 1:1–4; 6; 7:1–24). The essential "Gentileness" of Cornelius is further emphasized by Luke in Peter's retelling of the story in Acts 11. Peter does not even mention the fact that Cornelius is a God-fearer or that he has any relationship to the Jewish community. Both these facts would have been to his advantage, and the circumcision party would have had little objection to Cornelius's conversion (particularly in light of their acceptance of the Samaritans). Would this conversion have assumed the great importance it has as the turning point in the mission to the Gentiles if Cornelius was not indeed a true and complete Gentile?

All these concerns to find at least a quasi-Jewish connection for Cornelius (until recently he was even simply classified as a Jew) are textually inaccurate and are based more on a narrow and prejudiced understanding of *praeparatio evangelica* (preparation for the gospel), which does not allow a Gentile this privilege in the early church, without going through Judaism. This prejudice is present even today and reminds one of the debate in Tambaram, India, in 1938, between Hendrik Kramer (later echoed in Karl Barth) and P. Chenchiah (1886–1959), an Indian Christian theologian. The debate was, among other things, whether *praeparatio evangelica* was possible among people of other faiths outside of Judaism. Judaism and Christianity were *faiths,* and all others were simply *religions* and therefore had no presence of God till the proclamation by the missionaries.

The narrative in Acts 10:3 begins with Cornelius's vision of a visitation from an angel. The time of the vision (literally "the ninth hour of the day" or three in the afternoon) is also used to prop up the idea of his quasi-Jewishness, as it is the hour of Jewish prayers (Acts 3:1). Thus a quick assumption is made that Cornelius gets the vision while he was "observing this hour of prayer."[8] The text, however, merely states that the vision occurred at this time. The inference is perhaps drawn because of the reference to his constant prayers in 10:2 and 10:4. Cornelius sees the angel clearly — Luke makes it plain that there is no room for doubt or ambiguity. This is not a dream or a fantasy but a true epiphany. The angel calls Cornelius by name, which is reminiscent of many callings in the Old Testament, such as Hagar (Gn 16:8), Moses (Ex 3:4), Samuel (1 Sam 3:4–8), and so on. Cornelius responds to the angel in fear and refers to the one calling him as Lord, which is meant to be a generic theological assertion by Luke, in the vein of "the fear of the Lord is the beginning of wisdom" (Pv 1:7, 9:10; Jb 28:28; and Ps 111:10).

The Vision of Peter

The angel's response has produced equally problematic exegeses that implicitly assume Cornelius's quasi-Jewishness by drawing a parallel between his prayers and alms and the Jewish temple sacrifices.[9] This is

based on a continuing narrow hermeneutical exclusivity and fails to see
that God appears to him as an acceptance of his goodness. Is this a claim
that the presence of good works within Gentiles can act as a *praeparatio
evangelica?* Indeed it is! As Peter himself affirms in 10:34–35, "I truly
understand that God shows no partiality, but in every nation anyone who
fears him and does what is right is acceptable to him." It is clear that
piety is neither the gospel nor does it produce salvation in itself; rather,
the question in this case is of God reaching out and letting the gospel be
heard by a man who fulfills his own sense of righteousness/rightness and
piety. Notice that the proclamation here is presented as directly from
God and not through human agency.[10]

The angel's command is to send for Peter, who is residing in a tanner's
home in Joppa. Cornelius is not given a reason for this summons or
any idea of what to expect from Peter, yet he unhesitatingly fulfills that
demand as soon as the angel exits the scene. He calls "two of his slaves
and a devout soldier." It is interesting to note that Cornelius takes them
fully into his confidence — this is not just an order from a superior officer,
but an explained request. That he did this shows not only his level of
intimacy with them and his trust, but, more critically, he has to explain
what he has experienced and where they are going as a result of the
vision and the command of the angel. This is necessary because he is
sending them to a Jew, and one of the lowest social strata at that.

Both moves, from Caesarea to Joppa and from a centurion of the Italian cohort to a tanner's home, are a transition from absolute power and
might to the extreme periphery. Although he may have been approached
by God at the beginning because of his righteousness, the conversion
is only going to be possible when the periphery is the full transmitter
and bearer of the gospel. So here, even God who initiates the process
is unwilling to save the colonial power, however righteous it may be,
without direct intervention from the extreme periphery. This is clearly a
reflection of how human salvation begins by God's initiative but can be
fulfilled only by being located at the extreme periphery: a single mother;
in a manger with the animals and their excrement; and at Golgotha,
among the thieves outside the gate (see the description in Heb 13:12–
13). That Peter is staying with Simon the tanner is a clear indication
of Peter's own location in terms of his religious, cultural, social, economic, and political status. For it is clear that to be a tanner was to be
involved in a ritually impure and unclean profession; in Hindu terms

he was a *dalit,* and a wet *dalit* at that. Witherington rightly emphasizes that "tanners, because of their contact with the hides of dead animals, were considered unclean.... In fact the Mishnah and Talmud suggest they were despised because of their ongoing uncleanness caused by their trade..." (see *m. Ketub.* 7:10; *B. Pesah* 65a; *Qidd.* 82b).[11]

While Peter is praying he gets very hungry, and while the food was being prepared he falls into a trance (actually an ecstasy — *ekstasis*). Unlike Cornelius, who is fully conscious when he experiences the vision and sees it "clearly," Peter's vision takes place in a trance. He has his vision after Cornelius, in fact the next day. Luke is adamant in telling us that this is the second, not the first in the chain of events. This temporality in itself clearly hints at *praeparatio evangelica* for Gentiles.

Peter saw something like a large sheet descending. Again, Luke uses distinctly different language to depict the visions of Cornelius and Peter. Peter beheld (*theōrei from theōreō,* 10:11), whereas Cornelius saw (*eiden* from the verb *horaō,* 10:3). *Theōroi* were men who attended games, oracles, or sacrifices as public deputies or ambassadors on behalf of the *polis,* an action that has a clear resonance of *theos. Theōreō* thus gives the sense of an involved spectator,[12] whereas *horaō* has more the sense of intellectual knowing, a perception not sensual but of the soul — it "signifies not *'to have seen,'* but *'to know,'* "[13] and has a clear resonance of *eidos* — true forms, and thus eidetic knowledge. This may again reflect the different states in which Peter and Cornelius receive their visions. Peter, in a trance, experiences the vision like a spectator at an arena, whereas Cornelius clearly sees the angel and knows him. One is an ambassador of Christianity, both in the receipt of the vision and the proclamation of the gospel (see 2 Cor 5:19–26); the other is simply receiving a cognitive message.

While people have made different speculations about the meaning of the sheet,[14] I think the indication is that it is a specially designated sheet (thus pure) on which people eat and therefore has dietary implications, like the Persian and the Indian Muslims' *dastarkhwan.* To have ritually unclean food on such a sheet is already an aberration in that it denotes that all creatures are being made clean (*kosher*).[15] The clear intention of the vision is the inclusion of those who are officially designated as outside the *praeparatio evangelica.*

Having seen this inclusive vision, the consequential command is a simple "kill and eat," which has clear overtones of ritual sacrifice to be completed by eating.[16] It is exactly this combination that is abhorrent to Peter. First, the ritual sheet for food has been contaminated by unclean animals and now these unclean animals can be killed as part of a sacrificial ritual and be eaten. This would make even the most unclean Jew very queasy and disgusted.[17] There are therefore several layers of revulsion that Peter is battling simultaneously. His response, naturally enough, is an emphatic NO! Luke lets us know that Peter is clearly aware of who is commanding him — the *kurie* here is definitely a response to God, but he still has the nerve to turn him down. He is so bound by the Jewish dietary laws as part of his very being[18] that he is unwilling to listen even to God, who is commanding him and who in fact is the author of these laws according to the Jewish faith. This reminds me of the story of the fall in Islam where *Iblis* (Satan) is unwilling to prostrate himself before the human even though Allah has commanded him to do so. He is so monotheistic that he cannot obey even Allah, and so proud of his origin that bowing down to the human who is made of lesser stuff would be wrong (see *al-hijr* 15:28–34 and *al-araf* 7:11–13, and so on).

The Spirit rebukes Peter for his response and declares "what *God* has made clean *you* must not call profane." Whether this process of cleansing the unclean and profane things happens because they have been placed on the *dastarkhwan,* or because of the character of the command "kill and eat," or the combination thereof, what is clear is that it is being stated emphatically that the creatures are clean and kosher.[19] The command is repeated thrice and then the *dastarkhwan* is taken away without Peter ever obeying the command. Yet again Peter fails three times, harkening back to his denying Christ three times before the cock crowed (Lk 22:55–62 and parallels). The text lets us know that Peter simply doesn't understand the message that has been given to him. Why was the voice in the vision asking him to go against one of the fundamental tenets of Judaism, a tradition that in many ways served as an identification of Judaism under Gentile colonial rule?

In the meantime, the men from Cornelius have arrived and Peter is totally oblivious of their arrival, even though they are standing outside the house calling for him. Luke belabors Peter's complete inability or unwillingness to grasp the import of the vision's message. He is still befuddled and has to be nudged by the Spirit; there is no room for refusal now. The vision may have seemed ambiguous to Peter, but this command is not, especially given the information that "I have sent them." These are not just any Gentile visitors (although Peter doesn't know these details yet); they have been sent by God. Peter is being told in no uncertain terms that there is a divine agenda and agency in play here and he had better fulfill his role in it "without hesitation" (10:20). This time, Peter obeys immediately. One might add, somewhat cynically, that once a colonial Roman soldier is at one's door people listen even when they do not always listen to the voice of God!

There is absolutely no indication as to the religion of Cornelius's men, except that verse 2 states that "all his household" is both devout and God-fearing, which is further emphasized in the case of the soldier in verse 7. Interestingly, it is usually assumed that the visitors are Gentiles and therefore it could be said that Peter has already been influenced by the metaphorical invitation to inclusion in the most positive way and thus invites these men into the house of his host. This then begins the breakdown of the divisions between Gentile and Jews — a prefigurement of Peter's visit to Cornelius.[20] However, one could equally theorize that at least some of these men are Jewish and therefore they can make a robust case for Cornelius's highly pro-Jewish credentials. That they are not only invited in, but hosted and lodged overnight at a Jewish home with clear kosher practices (otherwise Peter's rejections in verses 13– 16 make no sense), at least implies their Jewishness.[21] Or perhaps, one might add more cynically, when the colonial power is at your door, ritual cleanliness was sacrificed or was sacrificeable!

These visitors present Cornelius's credentials (Acts 10:22). This is an expanded version of Luke's introduction 10:1–2. Now, rather than pious (*eusebēs*) he is righteous or just (*dikaios*), and a God-fearing man. Because they have come to a Jewish household and more important because they are inviting Peter to a Gentile one, they also present his credentials within the Jewish community: he is vouched for by the *whole Jewish nation*, not just by the local Jewish community. Overkill surely! This is not repeated in Acts 11 in the retelling of the story. What is fascinating is that those in power must justify themselves to Peter, even though Peter must have been himself quite frightened at the presence of these colonialists at his door. Their case for Cornelius undergirds our assertion that he is a Gentile. Hence, I have no idea on what grounds, except for restricting the *praeparatio evangelica,* anyone can assert that he is a Jew or a quasi-Jew.

The next day Peter leaves with the three visitors from Caesarea, accompanied by some of the believers from Joppa. There is no explanation as to why Peter feels the need to take them with him, but in 10:45 and again in 11:12 the text gives the impression that their primary role was to act as witnesses to the Jerusalem party. However, given that Peter was going as a solitary Jew to the house of a Roman colonial master, it seems probable that they went with Peter to provide security in case the colonial Roman officer turned nasty. With Peter as a guest in their community, they wanted to ensure that he had company if anything untoward were to happen there. They would be witnesses to such an event and could report back to the Jewish authorities.

When they got to Cornelius's home, he has also gathered his witnesses and has brought together a large group to watch over the meeting with the person the angel had recommended to him. Although Cornelius's vision was private, he has not, at any point, hesitated to share it with his household, family, and friends. This is definitely not a private meeting. Both sides are bringing witnesses to the event.

If there were still any lingering thoughts about Cornelius's Jewishness, what follows takes care of it. Cornelius does what no good Jew would ever do — he prostrates himself at Peter's feet and worships him, thus violating the Second Commandment and perhaps also the First. In a context other than the Bible, the Greek *prosekunesen* could simply mean courtly obeisance. In the New Testament, however, this word is used exclusively in a religious context, and in Luke it always means to worship.[22] Gaventa argues rather tritely that this isn't really as bad as it sounds, because "Cornelius may have confused Peter with the angel of v. 2...."[23] However, since Cornelius did not fall down and worship the angel in his first encounter, why should he begin to do so now? Such assertions, therefore, seem to be fairly strained if not totally false and are clearly based on the prejudice of making the *praeparatio evangelica* exclusive. The text here fully confirms Cornelius's Gentile credentials. This is firmly established in the very next verse where Peter responds strongly to Cornelius's worship by promptly commanding him to "stand up," and telling him that "I am only a mortal." This is a wonderful reversal: a colonized Jew of *dalit* status is ordering around a colonial master, a centurion of the Italian cohort!

The Gentile status of Cornelius is then further incontrovertibly established in 10:28 when Peter tells the many assembled that "you yourself know that it is unlawful for a Jew to associate with or to visit a Gentile." That a lower class/caste Jew is able to make such a strong statement against those who control the colonial power is similar to the prophetic proclamation that occurs several places in Acts (for example, 2:14ff, 7:1ff, and so on). Peter, then, goes on to explain that God's message has overcome his prejudice and even the law by which he lived. He has finally understood the point of the vision and the metaphor. After puzzling over it for a very long time, he has made the transition from the literal to the metaphoric — from food to people — both showing the necessary inclusion, which the church has still not fully come to terms with. Peter assumes that the assembled Gentiles all know about Jewish purity laws and thus how difficult it is for him to visit Cornelius. Yet he did this without objection once he understood God's inclusive command in the vision. Cynically, to rephrase a quote, "Methinks Peter doth protest too much" when he says "I came without objection"; was he going to object to the colonial soldier at his door and the command of the colonial master as he had to God's command? The ongoing fear and cowardice of Peter make me appreciate his humanness and his natural fear and yet respect his prophetic courage and political astuteness.

In response to Peter's question, "Now may I ask why you sent for me?" Cornelius more or less retells the story of his vision, with some embellishment. In both versions, however, what is important (perhaps particularly for Peter) is Cornelius's total lack of hesitation or questioning. Cornelius makes this gathering an explicitly religious occasion by asserting that "all of us are here in the presence of God to listen to all that the Lord has commanded you to say" (10:33). It is thus a *de facto* congregation waiting for the proclamation of the gospel through Peter. I agree with Witherington when he suggests that this may be a deliberate echo of Acts 1:13–14 where Jesus's disciples gather together in an upstairs room and pray: "[W]e are to see this story as the 'Gentile Pentecost,' the catalyst that would send forth a worldwide mission to Gentiles, just as Acts 2 indicated such a mission for Diaspora Jews and proselytes."[24]

What follows is yet another Petrine speech that may be termed a catechetical version of the gospel. It roughly follows the outline of Mark's gospel, beginning with the baptism of Jesus by John and the Holy Spirit, going through the healings and exorcisms, and ending with the crucifixion and resurrection. Peter goes on to give his credentials for evangelism,

announcing that he is a witness to Jesus's life, death, and resurrection —
he is one of those "chosen by God as witnesses" who "ate and drank
with him after he rose from the dead." This is his claim to apostleship.
Although he does not use the word here, it seems clear that these are the
credentialing parameters. Contrast this to Paul's claims of apostleship in
the epistles. This might explain why Luke, while holding Paul in very
high regard, never claims that he is an apostle.

Although Peter alludes to the Old Testament, he does not quote it
specifically as he does in some of his earlier speeches. Instead he stresses
that God "shows no partiality" and "in every nation anyone who fears
him and does what is right is acceptable to him"; in other words, he
has taken away the exclusivity and partiality of the covenant or the
covenantal law as a prerequisite (*praeparatio evangelica*) for the gospel.
Unfortunately, even today missiology is carried out with this exclusivity
and partiality.

Then the most unexpected and totally unanticipated inclusivizing oc-
currence takes place. "While Peter was still speaking, the Holy Spirit
fell upon all who heard the word" (10:44). Peter's evangelistic speech is
interrupted not by people coming forward and accepting Jesus as their
personal savior but by the appearance of the Holy Spirit, not just on
Cornelius, but on *all* who had gathered with him to hear Peter's message, and apparently on those who had come with Peter. Those who saw
themselves as the sole possessors of the Jewish covenant, law, and now
the gospel are first disturbed by this *laissez faire,* all inclusive *praeparatio evangelica* — God approaching the Gentile, a Jew going to a Gentile
home, proclaiming the gospel to the Gentile and not following the kosher
restrictions. Most offensive, however, is the Holy Spirit falling in an om-
nibus manner on all who are gathered and hear the gospel, even those
who are not circumcised. Not only do they receive the Holy Spirit (which
happens on a number of other occasions) but, worse still, they are all
speaking in tongues. They are obviously not happy at all with this. The
Greek word *existēmi,* translated here as astonished, actually would be
better translated as being "in a state or condition of consternation."[25]

At this point Peter poses a rhetorical question that also seems to seek
their *imprimatur* or *nihil obstat:* "Can anyone withhold the water for
baptizing these people who have received the Holy Spirit just as we
have?" (v. 47). However some questions need to be raised here. First,
who is the "we" to whom Peter is referring while mentioning the receipt

of the Holy Spirit? Is it those who accompanied him from Joppa, or the disciple in Acts 2? It is obviously the latter as is indicated in 11:15–17 where he makes a connection between this experience and the experience of the apostles in the beginning. He thus gives this occasion a very high status or, as some have called it, the "Gentile Pentecost."

The second question that arises is who was going to baptize them. It obviously was not Peter. The only ones able to do so would have been those who were in "consternation" at all the developments they have witnessed. They are now forced to baptize those whom they feel have no such right. But by doing this, they too are converted and become part of the team that stands by Peter in Acts 11 as part of his cohort against the circumcision party. After this Peter is invited to stay for several days and one assumes that he did so. Now his *dastarkhwan* is truly inclusive and he has a new *koinonia* that has become his home. All the impregnable borders have not only been crossed and destroyed, but the full implication of the gospel and the Pentecost for world Christianity has powerfully worked itself out.

Notes

1. Cornelius's conversion is also used as a justification for what Paul and Barnabas had achieved in Antioch, and Peter is acclaimed as the founder of the mission to the Gentiles, unlike Paul's claims in Galatians 2:7–8.

2. For a better understanding of where Samaritans stood vis-à-vis orthodox Judaism see Howard C. Kee, *To Every Nation under Heaven: The Acts of the Apostles* (Harrisburg, PA: Trinity Press International, 1997), 108; and Luke T. Johnson, *The Acts of the Apostles* (Collegeville, MN: Liturgical Press, 1992), 151.

3. In 82 B.C.E., P. Cornelius Sulla liberated ten thousand slaves, who then took his name or joined his clan. See especially Frederick F. Bruce, *The Acts of the Apostles: Greek Text with Introduction and Commentary* (Grand Rapids: Eerdmans, 1990), 252.

4. According to most scholars there were no legionary cohorts in Caesarea between 6 and 66 C.E., only auxiliary forces, usually made up of provincials, not Roman citizens (see Bruce, *Acts of the Apostles*, 252). There is a clear indication that an Italian cohort was stationed in Syria *after* 69 C.E. Scholarly opinion on this little detail falls broadly into three camps:

    a. Luke is providing historical legitimacy, but simply gets it wrong and/or mixes up a contemporary situation with the historical situation (see Hans Conzelmann, *Acts of the Apostles: A Commentary on the Acts of the Apostles,* trans. James Limburg, A. Thomas Kraabel, and Donald H. Juel [Philadelphia: Fortress Press, 1987], 81; and Gerd Lüdemann, *Early Christianity according to the*

Traditions in Acts: A Commentary, trans. John Bowden [Minneapolis: Fortress Press, 1989], 126);

b. Cornelius was from the Italian cohort in Syria, and had retired in Caesarea, the seat of Roman administration (see Kee, *To Every Nation under Heaven,* 130; and James D. G. Dunn, *Acts of the Apostles* [Cambridge: Epworth Press, 1996], 135); or

c. We do not know enough about the minutiae of Roman placements to dismiss the placement of an Italian cohort in Caesarea at this time, as the arguments against it are an argument from silence (see Ben Witherington, III, *Acts of the Apostles: A Socio-Rhetorical Commentary* [Grand Rapids: Eerdmans, 1998], 347; and Dunn, *Acts of the Apostles,* 135).

5. The best contemporary examples of such appointments are John Negroponte and Zalmay Khalilzad, who were both placed in charge of Iraq policy but were also full members of the State Department, to which they returned when their tenure was over. The former is now the deputy secretary of state and the latter is ambassador to the United Nations. Paul Bremer, on the other hand, who was presidential envoy to Iraq in 2003, did not come from an already existing status in the State Department and therefore did not have any position to return to.

6. Joseph A. Fitzmyer, *Acts of the Apostles,* Anchor Bible 31 (New York: Doubleday, 1998), 449–50.

7. See Charles K. Barrett, *Acts: A Shorter Commentary* (London: T&T Clark, 2002), 501; Conzelmann simply asserts that, "ὁ λαός, 'the people,' is used as a technical term for Israel" (*Acts of the Apostle,* 81); and Fitzmyer translates the text "He used to give many alms to the (Jewish) people" (*Acts of the Apostles,* 450). Kee, however, acknowledges it as "wider society" (*To Every Nation under Heaven,* 133).

8. Bruce, *Acts of the Apostles,* 253.

9. Ibid., 254; and Witherington, *Acts of the Apostles,* 348.

10. An interesting flip-side of this can be seen in 2 Kings 5, esp. vv. 15, 18, and 19.

11. Witherington, *Acts of the Apostles,* 333; see also Kee, *To Every Nation Under Heaven,* 126–27 and 136; and Bruce, *Acts of the Apostles,* 250.

12. Joseph H. Thayer, *A Greek-English Lexicon of the New Testament* (New York: American Book Company, 1889), 290.

13. Ibid., 173.

14. My favorite is the idea that Peter saw a sail on the horizon as he was dropping off (see Bruce, *Acts of the Apostles,* 255).

15. Gaventa completely misses the point when she asserts that Peter's response is "highly artificial"; he could have chosen one of the "clean" animals to eat. See Beverly Gaventa, *Acts of the Apostles* (Nashville: Abingdon Press, 2003), 165.

16. Barrett, *Acts: A Shorter Commentary,* 157. Although Conzelmann, Fitzmyer, and Bruce recognize that the word sometimes has that connotation, they all deny these overtones here (Conzelmann, *Acts of the Apostles,* 8; Fitzmyer, *Acts of the Apostles,* 455; Bruce, *Acts of the Apostles,* 255).

17. Unlike Barrett, *Acts: A Shorter Commentary,* 157.

18. Dunn, *Acts of the Apostles,* 137–38.

19. Gaventa states that "the subject is not [Peter's] practice, but his assumption that he knows what is clean and what is unclean," *Acts of the Apostles,* 166.

20. Kee, *To Every Nation under Heaven,* 138; Barrett, *Acts: A Shorter Commentary,* 159; Conzelmann, *Acts of the Apostle,* 82; Fitzmyer, *Acts of the Apostles,* 457; and Witherington, *Acts of the Apostles,* 351.

21. Witherington, *Acts of the Apostles,* 351.

22. Johannes M. Nützel, "προσκυνεω," in *Exegetical Dictionary of the New Testament,* vol. 3, ed. Horst Balz and Gerhard Schneider (Grand Rapids: Eerdmans, 1993), 173–75, see esp. 174.

23. Gaventa, *Acts of the Apostles,* 167.

24. Witherington, *Acts of the Apostles,* 354.

25. Frederick W. Danker, ed., *A Greek English Lexicon of the New Testament and Other Early Christian Literature,* 3rd ed. (BDAG) (Chicago: University of Chicago Press, 2000), 350.

4

CRITICAL BIBLICAL HERMENEUTICS
OF LI RONGFANG

In the Socio-Intellectual Context of China

ARCHIE C. C. LEE

The history of biblical scholarship in China in the first half of the twentieth century is a topic that has been neglected and buried at the early stage of its development because of the various cultural and political upheavals in China.[1] The Christian Bible reached Chinese shores in the shadow of the military and imperial conquests of the colonial expansion of the Christian world.[2] Ever since its first arrival, the Bible has never been a neutral and pure text representing the so-called good news of the Christian faith. It is very much a part and parcel of the colonial project. The "book" crosses geographical boundaries from the Western imperialistic world to the so-called uncivilized world of the pagans. The simplified and reduced form of the message of salvation of the soul persists and is believed to be valid and relevant for the colonized other. Translation, presentation, reception, and interpretation of it by Chinese Christian scholars in the multitextual, religiocultural traditions of China, and in the sociopolitical contexts of Chinese society, are important issues to look at in the cross-cultural interaction between China and the West. In the case of China in particular, the interpretation of the Bible is basically an encounter between what are essentially "two texts": the Christian Bible as a foreign import, and the indigenous Chinese religiocultural as well as the sociopolitical text. The former comes out of its Western habitat, crossing boundaries and trying to adapt to a new home in Asia. Its

70

imperial character shaped by the colonial legacy and a triumphalist mentality have, however, hindered the Bible from integrating into the new environment.

In this presentation, I will probe some of these issues and assess the biblical interpretation of Li Rongfang (Li Jung-fang, 1887–1965),[3] the first Chinese to undergo vigorous training in Western critical biblical scholarship and who received his Th.D. degree from Drew University in 1918. After returning to China, Li dedicated himself to the teaching of the Hebrew Bible at Yanjing (Yenching) University in Beijing, one of the earliest Christian universities established by missionaries in China. Besides introducing the current debates of biblical scholarship of his time, Li further appropriated the Hebrew Bible to the sociointellectual world of the May Fourth China. In addition to his published books and printed works, I am now in possession of the recently discovered manuscripts and handwritten notes of Li on biblical studies and related fields. This recent discovery of manuscripts will prepare the ground for the twofold purpose of my project: setting up an archive to preserve the fifty pieces of valuable manuscripts, making them accessible to scholars for future research, and conducting comprehensive research on Li's contribution to biblical interpretations in the context of China's quest for renewal and modernization in the midst of the East-West cultural encounter in the first half of the twentieth century. This paper is an initial attempt to assess Li's biblical interpretation based on the sixteen published articles on Genesis 1–11. The context of the May Fourth Movement of 1919 and the sociointellectual world of the so-called Chinese Enlightenment[4] will provide the hermeneutical framework for looking at Li's effort in border crossing. Though the conclusion drawn at the end of the essay is perhaps phrased rather negatively, it is hoped that it will enlighten us in the process of constructing and understanding biblical interpretation in border crossings in this volume dedicated to a scholar who has devoted himself diligently and contributed greatly to this arena of scholarly endeavor.

Li Rongfang and His Time

Li Rongfang was born on October 29, 1887, in Hebei Province. He received his primary education in a Methodist mission school in 1894 and was converted and joined the church in the same year. In January 1912, he graduated from Christian Peking University and attained an undergraduate degree with excellence in conduct and academic performance. After getting a master's degree in arts in 1913, he went to Drew University in the United States for further studies in Hebrew, Greek, and comparative religions. He graduated with a doctorate and the Golden Key Award in 1918. Li wrote his dissertation on the Egyptian Elephantine Papyri, which embodied the cultural adaptation and religious syncretism of the Jewish community in Egypt. During his graduate work, he spent most of his summer months in Chicago studying the Hebrew Bible and the archaeology of Palestine.

After returning to his country, Li chose to teach at his alma mater, Peking University, and was then appointed to Yanjing University. From the winter of 1926 to the summer of 1928, he served as dean of the School of Religion of Yanjing University. In 1953, the Yanjing University School of Religion merged into Yanjing Union Seminary. In 1961, he was elected as the committee member of the Second Chinese Christian Three-Self Patriotic Movement Committee. Li died on December 22, 1965, at the age of seventy-eight.

In the *Truth and Life Journal,* he published a number of articles related to biblical research on the Old Testament. These papers exhibited a wide range of interests with insights and academic acclaim. Furthermore, these articles were written in an easy, understandable style and exerted a fair amount of influence on the society at that time. Li was an outstanding biblical scholar of the first half of the twentieth century who received rigorous training in Western hermeneutics and can be said to have pioneered biblical research in the contemporary Chinese academic world. He was enthusiastic in his research, which he carried out with rigor. Many of his publications are serious interpretations of biblical texts, which serve as useful guides and references even for today's researchers. He had assimilated decades of learning, teaching experience, writing, collation, organization, translation, and editing to produce the first Hebrew-Chinese Dictionary in Chinese history.[5]

Well-versed in the academic pursuit of the archaeology of Palestine, he even made a trip to the Holy Land and explored the major archaeological sites on horseback with British and American experts in 1929.[6] His interest in the religious and cultural history of ancient Mesopotamia and Palestine inspired him to investigate the religious traditions of China.

From his manuscripts we discover that Li had done research and published on the religious tradition in the Chinese classics (*Shijing, Shujing, Yijing, and Liji*).[7] Li's impact can still be felt as he trained a number of first-rate biblical scholars in China, including Lu Zhenzhong, the foremost Old Testament scholar at Nanjing Theological Seminary, who single-handedly translated the entire Bible into Chinese and Xu Tingxin.

At a time when Western thought and knowledge were brought to China via the Western form of a higher education system, Li engaged Western biblical scholarship and applied it to the context of the intellectual world for national construction. Through him the Bible crossed borders from the imperial West to the colonized Chinese context together with Western liberalism, science, democracy, and evolutionism. These imported traditions and facets of the West impacted Li's interpretation of the Bible. Contemporary intellectual debates on the values of Chinese cultural and spiritual traditions and their proper place vis-à-vis Western forms of scientific advancement as well as a democratic political order presented a great challenge to the way Li located his biblical interpretation.

"Mr. Science" and "Mr. Democracy" have been regarded as the two most popular figures of the New Literary Movement and the May Fourth Movement of 1919 in China. They symbolize the attitude of some Chinese intellectuals toward modernization and Westernization. To these intellectuals these two aspects of Western culture were firmly believed to be of fundamental importance to nation-building and the social reconstruction of China. Chen Duxiu was credited with being the first Chinese intellectual to advocate the anticipated revolution to be brought about by democracy and science. In the declaration of the influential publication *Youth Magazine* (the name was changed to *New Youth* by the second issue), Chen first coined the above names for the two gentlemen.[8] There were, however, voices debating the foundation of Chinese culture and whether a renewal rather than a radical revolution could meet the challenges of the time. Was there anything at the core of the Chinese tradition, especially in its ethical system and its national spirit that could contribute to the radical transformation of China to the level comparable to that of the oppressive Western powers? To some intellectuals of the time the molding of a perfect moral selfhood[9] and personality, which would constitute the new national character of the Chinese nation, was of utmost significance to the future of China in the context of growing imperialistic pressure and military invasions.[10]

Debates surrounding the May Fourth Movement and its aftermath represent a hermeneutical quest for the proper understanding of China and her people vis-à-vis the Western powers and their civilization. Traditional Chinese culture and practices were under constant iconoclastic attacks. Despite the humiliations in the hands of the imperial colonizers, Western cultural achievement in science and democracy was upheld as the hope for the future of the Chinese nation. Western scholarship and its higher education system were introduced to Chinese education through the missionary boards and the establishment of Christian universities and colleges in China as well as in Japan.

Li can be better understood when he is located in the above socio-intellectual context. It is not surprising that the notion of democracy denoting the liberal spirit of Western culture, a critical scientific approach to knowledge, and a historical methodology characterize the scholarship of Li and his search for objective "truth." Li did not go along with the proposal of some for a total adoption of Western civilization and a radical rejection of Chinese culture. He tried to reexamine the material civilization of the West and reassess the value of the spiritual world embedded in it. He also devoted his attention and effort to Chinese classical texts and their spiritual content. To some of his contemporaries, the "old culture" was reactionary and burdensome. It seemed obstructive to the radical and progressive programs of renewal so needed for any future of the nation and its people. Li was in the support of upholding a third figure representing the current pet phrase of "Moral-Ethics Revolution" where "Miss Moral" was proposed as the third figure in addition to "Mr. Science" and "Mr. Democracy."

Wu Zhihuai was the first scholar who proposed to engage Miss Moral in order to deal with the internal matters of the Chinese nation and the inner spiritual well-being of one's personal life. To Wu, the two gentlemen, Mr. Science and Mr. Democracy, would be in charge of education and finance as well as politics and the welfare of the people respectively.[11] The spirit of the May Fourth Movement expressed itself in the dismantling of the old morality of traditional Chinese culture and in re-creating a new selfhood and moral character for humanity as the foundation on which the new social order could be established. This involved a new moral quality that did not depend on the old social value of filial piety, which favored feudalistic institutions and family structure. In this respect, what was advocated in the May Fourth Movement was individuality and *universum genus humanum*[12] or sovereign selfhood (*duli renge*) of the new human being. Confucianism and its hierarchical order, in which individuals do not exist independently, were therefore fiercely criticized.

The "Debate between Science and View on Life" in 1923 was the intellectual world's response to the faith crisis of the time. In Zhang Junli's lecture to the Tsinghua students held in February 1923 he further elaborated the queries of Liang Qichao on the omnipotence of science, and positioned the view on life in the spiritual sphere independent of science. This lecture created an uproar among the intellectuals in which science prevailed ultimately. Chen Duxiu's article entitled "Our Final Realization" in *Youth Magazine,* published on February 15, 1916, proposed to use a new ethics to oppose the old morality. Political revolution had to be followed by a revolution in ethics; otherwise, the reforms in politics would certainly bring conflicts if conservatism still held on to its social morals.[13] It is in this discussion about science and religion during the May Fourth period that Li Rongfang made a case for the value of religion and ethics with particular reference to those embodied in the Bible. In his interpretation of the Bible, Li crossed various borders from the ancient cultural world of the text, to its contemporary Western context, and eventually through his hermeneutical effort to the May Fourth China.

Li's Approach to Biblical Interpretation

Critical scholarship on the Bible had exerted its influence on Li. This is not surprising as he was well-trained by Drew University and by his liberal teachers who were deeply involved in the contemporary controversy of higher criticism in America. Among them, Robert W. Rogers (1864–1930), professor of Hebrew and Old Testament exegesis, was the most outstanding, although he was a controversial figure in the debates on higher criticism.[14] He was often accused of being a radical and looked at as one of those, such as S. R. Diver of Oxford.[15] Robert Rogers is well known for his work in west Asian archaeology and has written several definitive works, one of which is *A History of Babylonia and Assyria.*[16] Rogers and Li both took the position that the historicity of the biblical text was to be questioned and that the influences of the religious world of Mesopotamia and Canaan on the formation of the text must be duly acknowledged. It is therefore not unusual to read in Li's writings that the narrative materials in the Bible are "far from the historical fact" and have their origin in the neighboring countries of the people of Israel.[17] One example Li cites to illustrate this view is the creation stories in Genesis 1 and 2, the background of which is mainly Babylonian. Li understood and interpreted the so-called story of the Fall of Humanity and the Flood Story in the context and background of the Babylonian Enuma Elish and Gilgamesh Epic.[18]

The stories of Genesis 1:1–2:3 and 2:4–25 must be interpreted in their own time and context. Li recognized the historically and nationally conditioned character of the text. He insisted that a text cannot be understood properly if one removed the text from its original timeframe. Over and over he emphasized that the Bible was characterized by its ethnic "peculiarities."[19] Li tried to articulate biblical religiosity through the national thinking of his time. He asserted that the purpose of God's creation of humanity was for humans to develop as individuals and as social beings in a community. But eventually, God's plan was to see human beings cultivate their "selfhood" (*renge*) and enjoy well-being in the Garden of Eden.

In the interpretation of biblical religion, Li's major emphasis was on purifying the so-called lower-level religiosity in the Babylonian-Canaanite materials inherited from its cultural environment. His strong belief in the monotheistic faith of the Bible in its final form influenced him to posit a developmental view on the religion of Israel. There is a primitive stage in which the uncivilized and the savage elements and practices are recorded in the text. But there is also harbored in the biblical traditions a revealed truth that is eternal and universal. He set for himself the task of searching for the essence of this very "eternal truth" embodied in the present form of the text. The study of the creation stories in Genesis 1–3 fashions a good example of Li's methodology. In addition to the historical-critical biblical research, Li sought the ethical-moral dimension and the vision of personhood, selfhood, and perfect human nature embodied in the textual tradition of the Bible.

In one of the earliest articles Li contributed to *Truth and Life,* the journal of the School of Religion at Yanjing University, which bears the title "The Social Teaching in Early Hebrew Narratives," Li asserted that biblical studies must place emphasis on the ethics of the Bible. He distinguished between form and content when it comes to the literary text of the Bible and claimed that "the Hebrew people make use of all sorts of means to articulate their ethical views: discourses, law, practices and stories."[20]

Li placed great emphasis on the institution of family and underlined the significance of husband-wife relations. In the interpretation of Genesis 2 and 3, Li advocated that the family is not only a human organization but also a divine one ("an institution of God"). As God ordained the marriage institution in the Garden of Eden, God claimed that husband-wife relations therefore should "surpass the importance of father-son relations."[21] In this way, Li upheld his own biblical understanding and challenged the traditional Confucian ideology, which was under fierce debate at the time. The Confucian framework chooses to privilege father-son relations and exclude women from the five human relations that form the basic mode of behavior in society. The pecking order of a hierarchical society as advocated in Confucianism was based on ancestral worship, which required the male lineage to sustain the patriarchal orientation in traditional Chinese society. To Li, the husband-wife relationship superseded the priority ascribed to the father-son relations in the alleged writings of Confucius and Mencius.[22] Li's thoughts actually match much of what the new culture movement of the May Fourth period called for: anti-patriarchal (basing society on an egalitarian male/female relationship), anti-hierarchical relationships, and women's liberation.

Li's interpretation of Eve in the story of Genesis is worth pondering. To him, Eve knew what the "supreme good" was, but was nevertheless tempted to commit to doing the "lesser good." Li does not interpret the motivation of Eve's choice as between good and evil. She chose between the supreme good of obedience and a lesser good. The temptation came from the good look and good taste of the fruit of the forbidden tree. Li defines sin as falling into the temptation of something that is good and desirable, but that produces the consequences of adverse social effects: human alienation manifested in shifting responsibility on to others. He sees the life reality of sin and punishment as unavoidable and a necessity in the process of human evolution. Here one suspects that the heated contemporary debates in China and the West of his time on Darwin's evolution theory found their way into Li's discourse.

Li took Genesis 1 through 11 as containing stories of origin and etio-logical narratives. The beginnings of agricultural and pastoral activities are accounted for in the Cain and Abel episode in Genesis 4.[23] Indeed, the origin of city building, and the first practice of polygamy, the ances-try of the making of musical instruments and the invention of smithery also go back to the same passage (Gn 4:17, 19, 21, 22). The tradition has it that human beings are to call on the name of YHWH in the same chapter (Gn 4:26). As a critical scholar of contemporary scholarship, Li duly recognized the etiological function of this narrative and introduced it to Chinese readers of his time. The historicity of the story is definitely not Li's concern in his reading of this text.

In the interpretation of the Flood Story (Gn 6–8), Li further devel-oped his notion of a "clean society" in which moral excellence reigns supreme.[24] He argued that military power does not necessarily sustain a mighty nation. Only pure morals and superb ethics are the foundations for a strong and sustainable nation that brings well-being to human-kind. This, Li claimed, is the central thought promoted in the Flood Story. In Li's exposition of the patriarchal and Joseph stories, the lead-ing concept is that of the development of an appropriate selfhood and personality that will nurture the family, build up a harmonious society, and strengthen the nation. Abraham and Joseph become models of the ideal social teaching Li wanted to uphold for his times. The molding of altruism, "a personhood of putting the world first before individual interest" (*lishi renge*), is taken by Li as the key to a pure and superb morality.

The Table of the Nations (Gn 10) exhibits for Li the Chinese con-ception of the earth as one family and the brotherhood/sisterhood of humankind. The author of the Table puts all the nations and people known to him into an integrated familial network under the three sons of Noah. The idea of one common origin for all races under the one creator God, though not scientifically verifiable, enabled Li to advocate the value of the Chinese formulation of the principle of "One Family on Earth and the World Belongs to All." He saw the future hope for humanity in harmony in this very principle.

Yet Li endorsed a stereotypical approach to some of the biblical pas-sages. He went along with the Bible's way of romanticizing Israel and caricaturing the viciousness or wickedness of her enemies, especially the

Canaanites. Li followed this practice in his interpretation of the episode of the drunkenness of Noah. He interpreted Noah's curse of Canaan as being based on the assumed immoral life of the Canaanites. The political submission under the Semites and descendents of Japheth was assumed as a legitimate explanation for the curses. He asserted that "the purity of the religion of Israel is the reason for its blessedness."[25] The behavior of Shem was regarded as an expression of his filial piety. Li appealed to history as consequential evidence of the curses of Noah on the Canaanites, who were under the domination of Israel at the time of the writing of Genesis 9.[26] Li concluded that Genesis 9 is not a prediction of what will happen, but an explanation of historical reality. Through the episode, Li discerned moral lessons for his time. The great personal character of Noah saving human lives was affirmed, but Li warned against Noah's relaxed attitude after the Flood, which resulted in his lapse in morality and in committing the blunder of getting drunk. Li made use of the episode to admonish the necessity of exercising discretion and prudence, moral values emphasized in the Confucian teaching. He collected a whole list of sayings by Chinese scholars on the indispensable moral quality of circumspection to be developed and practiced especially in one's solitary living.[27]

Li showed great interest in other religions and expressed deep appreciation for the religious practices of Buddhism, Taoism, and Confucianism, the three major religious traditions that constitute the Chinese religious world and contribute to the various shapes and shades of Chinese cultural configurations. Li studied and wrote about these religious systems extensively. This interest in other religions was the result of his intense study of the religious world of West Asia. He intentionally aimed at interpreting the Bible in the religious context of China, but he could not transcend the limitations of his time. The supremacy claim of the Bible dominated his approach to the biblical text. For him the Bible was the central text, not one of many texts, in which the ideas and truth for renewal and the future of humankind were to be sought. He tried to cross borders from the historical context of the Bible to the contemporary context, in which the Bible was to be interpreted. But since Li's view of the eternal truth was embodied in the literary form of the West Asian religious world, he saw Chinese religions in the same perspective. He failed to give a proper place to the Bible in a multitextual environment of China, a question that is of great significance to Asian and Asian-American hermeneutics in general and Chinese biblical interpretation in particular.

We should, however, appreciate Li's effort to interpret the biblical text in the context of the Chinese cultural heritage. He advocated Confucian texts to be read together with comparable biblical passages. In the discussion on the punishment of Cain, Li distinguished between the human motivation in chastising criminals and the divine intention to reform sinners. The gift of a sign to Cain that he would not be killed by others (Gn 4:15) was interpreted as God giving Cain a chance to rehabilitate himself in his wandering. This point is supported by the Confucian idea of rehabilitating and forgiving rather then eliminating criminals.[28]

Yet Li was being burdened by the May Fourth Movement's discussion on the significance of scientific advancement for the building of China. He took the same position as some of his contemporaries in affirming that the principle of science was the measurement of modernity. With this understanding it is no wonder that Li, in his interpretation of Genesis, intentionally commented on the mythological nature of the materials in the text which may seem incredulous to the modern mind. The reference to the heroes of the pre-Flood narrative living for hundreds of years is a case in point.[29] In the spirit of science and scientific advancement, any element of superstition was always singled out and dismissed. Enoch, as the hero of the seventh-generation Hebrew ancestry, was understood by Li in light of the Babylonian parallels of the Sumerian King List. The character in the seventh generation had a special link with the Sun God and had been entrusted with the secrets of heaven and earth and the techniques of divination. The mysterious elements and superstitious character of the tradition were immediately disposed of as unscientific.[30]

To make sense of Enoch's walking with God (Gn 5:21, 24), Li emphasized the "ethical communion" and undermined all the superstitious colorings.[31] Genesis 5:29 is considered by Li as the center of the whole chapter. What is conveyed in the genealogy is the spiritual life that Li aspired to, the presentation of an ordinary life of giving birth, living to a certain age, and coming to the end of life in death. It is the life of divine fellowship, and a union with God. Li understood the marriage of the "sons of gods" and "the daughters of humankind" (Gn 6) in this context of divine-human union.[32]

For sure, Li's writing is a product of his times more than anything. In fairness to him, one has to read all his unpublished manuscripts before a comprehensive conclusive assessment can be made. In a positive sense, Li could be seen not as moralizing but rather deconstructing along the usual lines of iconoclasm. Perhaps what he attempted to find was a society not based on a fleeting ideology but rather on an ethical system that sustained and might lead to social stability. Li seems to try to show that the Bible embodies ethical and moral teaching that can nurture a citizen who is responsible and has a "humane personhood." He intended to co-opt the Bible and enable it to travel across cultures and sociopolitical contexts. He envisaged a good society not based on the rules of hierarchical order but on the responsibility of each individual. Considering that the Chinese traditional society was ordered mostly by birth and position, the call for individual responsibility was actually quite revolutionary.

Conclusion

Several aspects of Li's biblical interpretation merit our consideration. He has demonstrated good training and solid foundation in the historical-critical method. His interest in biblical scholarship and archaeological discoveries was unique at the time in China. He took upon himself the task of introducing Western scholarship of biblical studies to China. No doubt, he was basically a biblical scholar trained in the historical-critical methodology of his time. What was behind the text was his focus when he began to unravel a biblical passage. The Mesopotamian and Canaanite materials known to him were employed as the first step to approach the text. He was also familiar with and sensitive to the literary form and linguistic characteristics that constitute individual literary units of the Bible. He was not, however, just satisfied with constructing the "world behind the text" and the "world in the text." He attempted to address the "world in front of the text," to use the language of Ricoeur. The problem was the lack of a meaningful interactive depth between the three "worlds" of the text. For us, the vexed question in cross-cultural interpretation is whether Li was successful in engaging the Bible and its many contexts. Transposing the text to a new context and assuming its supremacy over other religiocultural texts simply does not come close to dealing with the complexity of cross-cultural hermeneutics.

Like all the other May Fourth intellectuals of his time, Li ventured into the quest for answers to the pressing issues of the Chinese context. He took upon himself the burden of providing a viable solution to the burning question of his age: saving the nation by launching an ethics/moral revolution that replaced the traditional moral teaching. In spite of his training in critical biblical scholarship, he allowed the text to adapt to the contextual demand of nurturing an independent selfhood for the salvation of the nation. He went along with the contemporary jargon of the intellectuals and accepted the May Fourth ideology. The agenda of nationalism and modernization seemed to dominate his thinking and his concern. He acknowledged that biblical literature embodies the cultural form of the ancient West Asian literary tradition, through which the "eternal truth" is being manifested. The Bible was used as a moral book — at times an "imperial and supreme book" — superseding the native ethnical values and moral ideals. It was assumed to fill the moral vacuum of the time and contribute to the nation-building project.

Methodologically speaking, Li's was not really a contextual reading of the Bible. In the end, the context dictates and dominates. Instead of the text inspiring the context, the context, which in actuality is full of texts and a text in itself, sheds light on the text. The anticipated dialogical mode of interaction between "text" and "context" is suspended. What remain are independent historical-critical and literary studies of the text on the one hand and a reading of "eternal truth" superficially applicable to the context of the time. Furthermore, Li's reading does not match the criteria set forth in cross-textual interpretation, which give an equal status to both the biblical text (Text B) and the Asian (Text A).[33] Li's is an example of applying the message of the Bible to a new context. In cross-cultural interpretation, the vexing question is whether Li was successful in engaging the Bible and its many contexts. Transposing the text to a new context and assuming its supremacy over other religiocultural texts simply does not come close to dealing with the complexity of cross-cultural hermeneutics.

As an intellectual who tried to enable the Bible to cross borders and engage with China, Li, like most of the May Fourth Chinese intellectuals, was unable to shake off the nation-building project and therefore could not be critical of the moral burden of modernization of China.[34] He had yet another burden to carry and that was his "obsession with the Bible," defending the ethical supremacy of the biblical text. He found in the biblical texts the solution to the problem of China and co-opted it for the nation-building project. In doing so, he reduced the richness and plurality of the biblical tradition to just a few ethical principles of "eternal truth."

Notes

1. This essay is a partial result of the project funded by an earmarked grant from the Research Council of the Hong Kong Special Administrative Region, China (CUHK4712/05H).

2. Brian Stanley, *The Bible and the Flag: Protestant Missions and British Imperialism in the Nineteenth and Twentieth Centuries* (Leicester: Apollos, 1990) and Joseph Tse-Hei Lee, *The Bible and the Gun: Christianity in South China, 1860–1900* (New York: Routledge, 2003).

3. This essay follows the system of transliteration of Chinese characters adopted in China.

4. Vera Schwarcz, *The Chinese Enlightenment: Intellectuals and the Legacy of the May Fourth Movement of 1919* (Berkeley: University of California Press, 1986).

5. The draft was personally handed over to Nanjing Theological Seminary years ago by his wife, Shi Yueqing. Scholars are eagerly awaiting its publication.

6. Li Rongfang, "Record of Exploration in the Holy Land," *Truth and Life* 4, nos. 7–8 (1929): 16–24 and 4, no. 11 (1930): 16–29.

7. These are among his unpublished manuscripts in the author's possession.

8. See Lin Yü-sheng, *The Crisis of Chinese Consciousness: Radical Antitraditionalism in the May Fourth Era* (Madison: University of Wisconsin Press, 1979).

9. Selfhood incorporates the Western notion of individuality (worth of the individual).

10. See discussion and analysis in Chow Tse-tsung, *The May Fourth Movement: Intellectual Revolution in Modern China* (Stanford, CA.: Stanford University Press, 1967 [1960]) and *Research Guide to the May Fourth Movement; Intellectual Revolution in Modern China, 1915–1924* (Cambridge: Harvard University Press, 1963).

11. Wu Zhihuai, "Cosmology and View of Life in a New Form of Belief," *Science and Life* (Shanghai: Shanghai Bookstore, 1925), 135–36.

12. The Chinese notion of *renge* can be understood and translated by Francis Bacon's Latin expression of *genus humanum*, often also used as *universum genus humanum*, which supports the conception of the "New Human Being" during the May Fourth Movement. For discussion of the concept, see Roman Malek, *"Renge: Ergänzung oder Ersatz der konfuzianischen Konzeption des junzi? Zu einem Versuch aus den ersten Dekaden des 20. Jahrhunderts"* (trans. into Chinese) in *Symposiums-Beiträge: Drittes Internationales Sinologisches Symposium der Katholischen Fu Jen Universität: Personen — und Individuumsbegriff in China und im Westen — Der Beitrag der Bonner Sinologischen Schule um Professor Rolf Trauzettel* (Taipei: Fu Jen University Press, 2006), 232–57.

13. As "Mr. Science" was in general a symbolic banner in the May Fourth Movement, religion was therefore regarded as the object of total negation. The struggle did

not cease from the Anti-Confucian Movement of 1916 to the Anti-Christian Movement of 1919, and then through the establishment of the Great Alliance against Religions in 1922. There was a proposition of modernism that advocated the abolition of religions such as Confucianism, Buddhism, Taoism, and Christianity. The slogan of "replacing religion with science" was put forward by academics in their anti-religion stance. However, the "New Youth" and the "New Tide Association" did not share the same understanding. In the expression of the "New Youth," science was used to regulate the relationships between human beings and nature, human beings and society, and human beings and history. The science the "New Tide" talked about was more about a research method, calling for a certain degree of freedom in thinking. They recognized that science could not solve all of life's problems. They thought that when there were upheavals in society, political crisis, and cultural degradation, there would be a more urgent need for faith that could support people's ideas and action. The New Tide Association had shown great interest in religions, especially in Buddhism and Christianity.

14. Robert William Rogers arrived at Drew in 1893 to fill the chair in exegetical theology. He had received his B.A. from the University of Pennsylvania in 1886, a second B.A. from Johns Hopkins, and a Ph.D. from Haverford in 1890. He had an international reputation for scholarship in his definitive work on Babylonian and Assyrian history and their religions. He published fourteen books, all of which can be found in the library of Drew University.

15. In his Matriculation Day Address in 1920, Robert Rogers gave his position paper "The Old Testament," which was later published in the Drew University Seminary Bulletin. He was criticized by lay people and leaders of the Methodist Church. See the short article in *Eastern Methodist* 5 (1920): 2–3.

16. The book was first published by Eaton & Mains in New York in 1910 and then revised and enlarged by Abingdon Press in 1915. Another of his books is *The Religion of Babylonia and Assyria: Especially in Its Relations to Israel: Five Lectures Delivered at Harvard University* (New York: Eaton & Mains; Cincinnati: Jennings & Graham, 1908).

17. Wu, "Cosmology and View of Life in a New Form of Belief."

18. Li provided a long comparison of the Flood and the so-called Babylonian Flood Story in the Gilgamesh Epic.

19. Li Rongfang, "The Origin of Humanity and the First Couple," *Truth and Life* 9, no. 8 (1936): 474.

20. Li Rongfang, "The Social Teaching in Early Hebrew Narratives," *Truth and Life* 5, no. 1 (1930): 35.

21. Ibid., 36.

22. Mencius, King Tang I.

23. Li Rongfang, "Cain, the Criminal," *Truth and Life* 10, no. 2 (1936): 75.

24. Li, "The Social Teaching in Early Hebrew Narratives," 39.

25. Li Rongfang, "The Drunkenness of Noah," *Truth and Life* 10, no. 6 (1936): 351.

26. Ibid.

27. Ibid., 348–55.

28. Li, "Cain, the Criminal," 82.

29. Li Rongfang, "Personae before the Flood," *Truth and Life* 10, no. 3 (1936): 133–34.

30. Ibid., 135.

31. Ibid., 135, 139.

32. Ibid., 140.

33. Archie C. C. Lee, "Biblical Interpretation in Asian Perspective," *Asia Journal of Theology* 7 (1993): 35–39.

34. Xia Zhiqing (C. T. Hsia)'s notion of "obsession with China," making China the burdensome context for every interpretation, is a leitmotif throughout the twentieth century; see C. T. Hsia, "Obsession with China: The Moral Burden of Modern Chinese Literature," in *A History of Modern Chinese Fiction 1917–1957*, 3rd ed. (Bloomington: Indiana University Press, 1999), 536.

PART TWO

THEOLOGICAL PERSPECTIVES

5

LET GOD BE GOD

Crossing Boundaries
as a Theological Practice

M. Thomas Thangaraj

The pioneering role of R. S. Sugirtharajah in opening up Asian Christian scholarship to non-Asian readers is recognized all over the world. Two things stand out as I reflect on my friendship with Sugirtharajah, which began in 1974 when we were students in the Master of Theology Program at the United Theological College, Bangalore, India. Sugi has been "postcolonial" himself from the time I first knew him. He was breaking new ground in Indian theological thinking and Indian biblical interpretation with his critical approach to the past, his comprehensive understanding of the contemporary context, and his vision of an egalitarian community of scholarship. I worked closely with him when the faculty of Tamilnadu Theological Seminary, under Sugi's leadership, was constructing a contextual curriculum for the Bachelor of Divinity students during the later part of 1970s. As I look back on that experience, I can detect the stamp of postcolonialism in the very construction of that curriculum. Second, Sugi is one of the persons who opened my eyes to recognizing theological resources far beyond the narrowly Christian and scholarly materials. His familiarity with the popular literature in Tamil, especially secular magazines and novels, was a challenge to all of us as we attempted to construe ways of thinking theologically in Tamil. He was indeed crossing borders in terms of biblical exegesis and theological method. I consider it an honor and privilege to contribute this essay as we celebrate his work.

I wake up every morning to the call to prayer by my Muslim neighbors in the town of Palayamkottai in South India. The Muslim cantor begins by repeating four times the proclamation, *Allahu Akbar,* God is great. This call is definitely a summons to acknowledge the greatness of God and thus let God be God! My Hindu neighbors, on the other hand, affirm the greatness of God in a totally different manner. They never fail to quote a verse from the earliest Hindu scripture, namely, the *Rig Veda*. It claims, "Truth is one; sages call it by many names." According to this verse, Being or Truth is such a limitless One that all names and forms that we ascribe to it can never exhaust its vastness. Here again is a call to let God be God. The Ten Commandments given by Yahweh to the Hebrew people at Mount Sinai begins with this: "I am the Lord your God...you shall have no other gods before me" (Ex 20:2, 3). The Deuteronomic commandment expresses the same in the following manner: "Hear, O Israel: The Lord is our God, the Lord alone. You shall love the Lord your God with all your heart, and with all your soul, and with all your might" (Dt 6:4). Later, the prophet Isaiah puts it this way: "I am the Lord, that is my name; my glory I give to no other, nor my praise to idols" (Is 42:8). These verses, together with the opening declaration of God as the creator of heaven and earth, point to the greatness of God and instruct us to let God be God. [As we examine the various religious traditions of the world, we are bound to discover that the call to let God be God is present in many traditions, though in differing forms of articulation.]

The Christian theological tradition, as well, has a strong emphasis on the Godness of God and the limitations of our human perceptions and understandings of God. Jesus, in his own teachings and ministry, emphasized the greatness of God by calling his followers to "love God with all your heart, with all your soul, with all your mind, and with all your strength" (Mk 12:30). Christian theologians over the centuries have highlighted the transcendence and greatness of God in their writings. Karl Barth, a leading Protestant theologian of the twentieth century, did make a clarion call to let God be God. Theologian Timothy Gorringe sees Barth's theological project as "against hegemony," which is the subtitle of Gorringe's book.[1] As he puts it: "It is because Barth's theology, from first to last, is an attempt to witness to *this* God (the One who is not identical with any ideology) that it resists all attempts to find interpretative master keys, which would again bring it under theological-cultural hegemony."[2] In outlining the purpose of the church and its ministry, H. Richard Niebuhr engages in an exposition of the meaning of one's love of God and love of neighbor. Idolatry, for Niebuhr, is our "confusing proximate with ultimate goals."[3] He goes on to relativize, in the name of God, church denominations, biblical writings, and even Christological articulations, and demands that, while we recognize their importance in our love of God and neighbor, we should not turn them into "substitutions of the proximate for the ultimate."[4] A contemporary American theologian, Gordon Kaufman, dealing with the "Principle of God's Absoluteness," has this to say:

> The "ultimate point of reference," as that to which every item of experience and every object within the world, as well as the world itself, is to be related, transcends all experience and the world and may not be confused or identified with any item of experience or object in the world.[5]

How do we translate this declaration — Let God be God! — and allow it to take concrete expression in our lives? How do we transform our theological articulation into a theological *practice?* I suggest, in this essay, that crossing boundaries is a way to go about translating our "theology" into a theological "practice." I maintain that when we cross boundaries, whether cultural, linguistic, religious, or musical, we are engaged in theological practice. I wish to use my own boundary-crossing experiences as a heuristic tool to establish this claim. Therefore, let me first begin with my experience of boundaries.

As far as I can remember, my life began as a little boy in a remote village in Tamilnadu, India, called Kadayanodai. The boundaries were very clear to me at that time. I was a Christian, living in a Christian village, with St. Thomas's Church at the center of the village. This meant that we had clearly defined boundaries between us and the Hindus in the neighboring villages. I experienced a crossing of that boundary only a few times. When I was an eight-year-old boy I went to a nearby village called Kurankani to witness the annual Hindu festival. Also, when I was in elementary school I went on an excursion to Tiruchendur, a Hindu pilgrimage town. Otherwise, the boundaries were very clear. Moreover, I was a Tamil Christian; that meant I spoke Tamil, a Dravidian language, which also defined boundaries. I could not understand when my parents spoke to each other in English in order to keep secrets from me and my sister. When I entered sixth grade, I began to learn the English language, and only then I began to cross linguistic boundaries. I was a Tamil Christian who belonged to the Church of South India.[6] This meant that I sang mostly Western hymns (translated into Tamil) and some local hymns set to Indian music. I had no familiarity or understanding of the South Indian classical music called Carnatic music. My musical repertoire was very limited and operated within narrow boundaries. Furthermore, my cultural milieu was governed mostly by the subcaste I belonged to and the Christian church of which I was a member. There were explicit and implicit boundaries to my social interactions and behavior. For example, our community, both within the church and outside, operated with gender segregation. It was only when I moved from Kadayanodai to other places in Tamilnadu and later to other towns in India, and finally to other parts of the world that I began to cross several more boundaries. These crossings appeared more like accidents, adventures, or journeys to me at that time. But today I see them as instances of "theological practice." I have chosen three types of boundary-crossing experiences that throw light on the theological practice of letting God be God.

Crossing Cultural Boundaries

The culture of Tamil Christians during my boyhood was distinctively gender-segregated. Only in elementary schools were boys and girls together in class. Otherwise, there were separate schools for boys and for girls. Similarly there were men's colleges and women's colleges. During worship in the church, the men sat on one side of the aisle and the women on the other. Even in family gatherings one would notice that men and women socialized in separate groups. From such a gender-segregated setting I moved to Serampore College in West Bengal to pursue my theological studies.

I was surprised to find that men and women studied together in the same college and the interaction among men and women was much freer than I had known in my home area. I joined the local church choir, which was made up of men and women. Only a few of us were non-Bengalis. After one of the rehearsals, one of the young Bengali women in the choir invited me to go to her home the following weekend. Such an invitation from a young woman would never have happened in my hometown.[7] I did not know what to make of it. Would her parents be there when I dropped in? Would they approve? Was it right to take the invitation seriously and go at all? These questions haunted me the whole week. Finally, I gathered courage and went to her home that weekend. As I approached her home, I saw her parents waiting at the door to receive me and to offer me their most generous hospitality. I had crossed a cultural boundary I had lived by all my life!

While I was a doctoral student at Harvard, a very interesting event took place that highlighted again the crossing of cultural boundaries. On January 21, 1981, I remembered that my daughter was celebrating her fourth birthday that day. Since I was living alone in the dormitory while my family was in India, I decided to celebrate my daughter's birthday in the same manner as she would back in India. The birthday child is supposed to take a tray with candies to her neighbors, and as they see her with candies they would ask, "What's the matter?" The child would say "It's my birthday!" They would pick up a candy and wish her all the best for her birthday, and perhaps give her a gift of money. So I had a tray with candies and went to my dorm mates. The first person I met looked at the tray and said, "No, thank you!" and walked away. Three more persons had the same response. When I approached the fifth person, I said: "Please take a candy and ask me 'What's the matter?' " He did, and I was able to tell him about my daughter's birthday and celebrate with him. My American friends belonged to a culture where when presented with a tray of candies they would ask themselves "Do I want a candy?" If they do not, a polite "No, thank you" is an appropriate response. In our Indian culture, however, the situation demands that I give absolute attention to the person in front of me and therefore need to ask "What's the matter?" Indian culture demands that I take a candy even when I do not *want* or *like* candy. To refuse to take a candy is to reject any relationship with that person.[8]

Relativization of Culture

Both these incidents made me aware of who I was in a world of many cultures. Crossing cultural boundaries does make us intensely self-conscious. We come to discover the distinct features of our own culture and our own identity. The differences awaken in us a strong sense of self. As we keep crossing boundaries, we begin to grow in such self-awareness and we begin to understand how we have been shaped, formed, and influenced by our own culture. But at the same time, we begin to discover the nuances of the culture of the other. As Martin M. C. Yang writes, "It is often said that members of a minority are more conscious than others of both their values and those of the majority."[9] Such a heightened awareness of differences releases one from a value-biased view of culture. The use of the word "cultured" to mean "civilized" is truly a value-biased view of culture. Only in such a view can one talk about superior culture and inferior culture.

When such an awareness of self comes into being, two theological practices emerge. First, the very act of self-awareness is a theological practice in itself. Is it not the case that one of the tasks of theology is to locate oneself in the ultimate context of the Divine? In thinking about God, every theologian engages in an exercise of discovering the place of all humans, especially the theologian himself or herself in relation to God. A strong sense of the self that refuses to limit itself to the boundaries of any one particular culture is, in fact, an acute awareness about one's location in the ultimate context of all existence, namely, God. Each time we cross cultural boundaries, we place ourselves in a bigger context than that of our own particular culture. For example, in inviting me to her home, the young woman in Serampore helped me to cross my boundary and place myself in a larger context. The celebration of my daughter's birthday with my American friends offered me an occasion to transcend my cultural boundaries and see myself in a larger world of many cultures. Precisely at these moments, theology functions as an exercise in self-awareness and self-knowledge.

Second, one is also led to an acknowledgment of intercultural differences without hegemonic claims about either one's own culture or that of the other. Recognition of differences, in fact, frees one from a value-biased view of culture. Of course, we cannot escape the question of value when we cross boundaries. For example, is gender segregation a matter of ultimate value? Does a lack of gender segregation enable expressions of genuine freedom? Yet our answers to these questions do not come from the safe and secure location of our own culture; they confront us only when we actually cross our cultural boundaries. We stand on the boundary, so to speak, and face these questions. Therefore, even when we ask these questions, our experience of crossing boundaries prevents us from making any hegemonic claims about either our own culture or the culture of the other. When we reject hegemonic claims, we are involved in a theological practice — a practice that questions and relativizes everything that is. In other words, when such relativization happens, one is truly affirming and claiming "Let God be God!"

Crossing Religious Boundaries

Religion, for our purposes here, may be understood as consisting of five elements: conduct, culture, community, *cultus,* and creed. We may see them as forming concentric circles with creed at the center and conduct as the outermost circle. Each of these elements has its own boundaries. Religions do operate with a code of conduct or a set of ethical norms, and these have their own boundaries. For example, in the Jain religious tradition, violence of any kind is outside the boundary of ethical behavior. Similarly, one can discover boundaries with regard to the culture that surrounds a particular religion and gives a public form to it. The architectural peculiarity of mosques throughout the world illustrates a cultural boundary. In the same way, one cannot envision a religious community without setting up boundaries. Church, within the Christian tradition, has definite requirements for membership and thus boundaries are clearly drawn. Similarly, in the areas of worship and beliefs one can easily detect limits and boundaries. The concepts of clean and unclean and the accompanying kosher laws illustrate some of the boundaries that govern the Jewish religious tradition.

I mentioned earlier how religious boundaries during my childhood were clearly defined. For example, we were not supposed to enter Hindu temples. That would be seen as a breach of our loyalty to Christianity. Therefore, my intentional visits to Hindu temples began to happen much later when I developed a friendship with Dr. S. Gangadharan, a Hindu scholar and colleague under whom I studied the philosophy of Tamil Saivites,[10] called Saiva Siddhanta. Gangadharan and I have visited several times the Meenakshi Amman Temple at Madurai, South India. As we approach the inner sanctuary of the temple, we notice a sign board that reads: Only Hindus Allowed Beyond This Point! This was put up to maintain a worshipful atmosphere in the central shrine of the temple. Ganga would choose not to go into the inner sanctuary for my sake; rather he would fall prostrate on the floor toward the shrine and pray. My own religious boundaries, however, would not permit me to pray like him; I could only stand next to him and utter a silent prayer, thanking God for Ganga's friendship. During those earlier visits to the temple, I had not fully crossed the religious boundary. Now, however, after several years of such encounters and visits, I find myself crossing that boundary. When I take my students from the Candler School of Theology at Emory University to the Hindu Temple of Atlanta, I stand right inside the inner sanctuary before the image of Vishnu (in the form of Venkateswara). At those moments I feel the presence of God and am able to join in the *puja* (worship) with reverence.

Relativizing Religions

When one crosses a religious boundary, a person can develop a "kenotic" (emptying) posture that enables one to be a gracious and grateful receiver of glimpses into the Divine. Here is a theological practice that relativizes one's own vision of God and lets God be God even in places where one does not expect to encounter God. In the name of God, one accepts the status of a stranger. Anthony Gittins writes, "To embrace the status of a stranger is to empower other people and to dare to infuse some trust into a world where self-interest and suspicion seem to walk unimpeded."[11] Giving an opportunity to the other to act as the host offers them an occasion to be the subjects of history. That is how the kenotic posture expresses itself in the crossing of religious boundaries.

Moreover, one is led to an acknowledgment and celebration of one's spiritual journey without hegemonic claims about the nature of the destination. We know the journey but we are yet to reach the destination. There are certainly varied views on the destiny of the human spirit; we all have our own views of "salvation." In other words, the goal of human life is, indeed, understood in very many ways.[12] Yet when we cross religious boundaries, we are led to acknowledge that it is the journey that matters. It is the journey that is common to us, even when our vision of the destination is very different. Such a journey relativizes our own views of both human destiny and the destiny of the universe and lets God be God.

When the journey matters, the conversation on the way becomes important as well. It is not like a race where what is most important is reaching the finish line first. This is a walk, a journey where the conversation on the way is the most significant part of the journey. Christian theologians have, all along, seen conversation as a theological practice. To cite one example, St. Anselm's writings, including *Cur Deus Homo,* exemplify this theological practice.[13] In the theological practice of conversation, "no single voice can lay claim to (religious truth), for each understands that only in the ongoing conversation as a whole is truth brought into being."[14] We do hear behind this conversation a bold proclamation: Let God be God!

pluralism?

Crossing Musical Boundaries

The last two crossings focused on the centrifugal movement of my border crossings — a movement from a narrow circle to a wider one. As far as music is concerned, my movement was centripetal — a movement from the periphery to the center. My musical life started with Western music. I was a member of the church choir from the age of eight. I learned to play the organ at home under the instruction of my mother, who was a reasonably good organist. My training took me only to the level of playing simple hymns. The hymn that I played so often at that time was "Sun of My Soul, My Savior Dear." It was a piece of music with a simple melody and even simpler harmonization. Thus I grew up with Western music in its simplest forms. The major and minor chords gave me a sense of order and harmony. I used to harmonize Indian musical hymns on my own and play them on the organ. When we sang such Indian hymns in our churches, we sang them most often with a flavor of Western music and with a good dose of Western harmony. Western music, especially with its four-part harmony, was seen as an important way of defining one's affiliation with the Christian faith. The first Tamil hymn that I ever wrote and set to music is an excellent example of such simple Western harmony. It was set in F Major with a waltz rhythm and operated purely with the three chords — F, B-flat, and C-seventh. Once when I played a recording of it to an American couple who were visiting our home, they spontaneously stood up and danced to the waltz rhythm!

My interest and involvement in South Indian classical music began much later in my life. I learned to play the violin from a Carnatic music teacher in Palayamkottai and later studied vocal music under the patronage of Srinivasa Iyengar, a well-known classical musician in Madurai, South India. While learning from him, I realized that I was beginning to cross my musical boundaries and to enter a different world of musical sensibility. It was an experience of going to the roots of my Indian heritage and discovering a music that resonated with me at the depths of my existence. Such a discovery led me to celebrate the rich tradition of South Indian classical music and to venture to use them profusely in my hymnody. While singing the Tamil hymns set to classical music, I experienced a recovery of the deep recesses of my linkage to the Divine. The experience of the Divine could no longer be limited to Western hymns and music!

Relativizing Music

How is this experience a theological practice? Crossing musical boundaries opens oneself to the depths of one's longing for and resting in the Divine. I came to see the South Indian classical music not simply as a significant part of my cultural heritage but most of all as an occasion to encounter the Divine. Don Saliers, a church musician and theologian, and Emily Saliers, a folk-rock singer and one of the *Indigo Girls,* have written a book about their experiments with music. They open the book by saying, "Each of us has known echoes of a transcendent reality in and through music."[15] After narrating and reflecting on their experiments with music, the Saliers end their book by writing,

> Begin with the music you already cherish but live with openness to the possibility that in the coming years music you have not heard will lead you more deeply into the mystery at the heart of all that is....If you awaken to the search for God, may you hear in some unexpected music that God is seeking you.[16]

This is exactly what happens when one crosses musical boundaries. One is found by God. "Let God be God" happens all over again.

I begin every class session in the courses I teach at the Candler School of Theology by singing a song together. When I taught a course titled "Doing Theology in the Global Context," I composed a song for us to sing together before every class session. The text for that song comes from St. Augustine's *Confessions,* and the tune is set to a South Indian melody and rhythm. The text is: "You have made us for yourself, O God; our heart is restless until it rests in you." When my students sing this text in an unfamiliar melody and to a much more unfamiliar rhythm (seven beats in a bar), they are led into a new experience of the presence of God. Their theological exercise becomes an adoration of God. The Indian melody accompanied by the drone (*sruti*) creates a different sense of harmony, and the melody transports them to an unknown territory. Just like the way I crossed musical boundaries in my life, my students experience a crossing through the singing of this song.

There is an experience of reconciliation and a fresh understanding of harmony that emerge out of this experience of crossing musical boundaries. My view and appreciation of harmony have changed over the years. The harmony that happens in the South Indian music has opened my eyes to recognize harmony in all its varied forms. As any student of South Indian music knows, it is basically melodic and has no organized or planned harmony. Yet since the melody is sung to the accompaniment of the drone (*sruti*), which sustains the first and fifth notes of the scale (*raga*), harmony emerges in differing forms through the singing of the piece. At times it may sound discordant to Western musical ears. However, the crossing of musical boundaries leads one to an acknowledgment and experience of living with instances of discord without hegemonic claims about harmony. Such moments of recognition can truly be called "theological" moments since they relativize our notions of harmony and thus let God be God.

Relativizing Boundaries

Let me conclude by returning to the question of boundaries again. Boundaries have three distinct functions. In our earlier discussion of cultural, religious, and musical boundaries we did note these three functions. Let me elaborate on them and see how the very crossing of boundaries is a process of relativization that ultimately leads us to the theological practice of letting God be God.

1. Boundaries can be understood "as markers for one's individual and communal identity."[17] When we examined the experience of crossing cultural boundaries, we did notice how our identity is reshaped and re-formed in newer ways. Our border-crossing helps us to respect and promote a distinctive identity and, at the same time, appreciate and celebrate "otherness" as well. This requires a realization of the fragility of the boundaries that mark our identity, and a realization of the proximate character of one's identity.

2. Boundaries can be viewed as "barriers to fence out other people different from oneself."[18] When we discussed the crossing of religious boundaries, it was clear that the type of Christian faith I was brought up with operated precisely with an intention to keep people who do not belong to the Christian faith outside one's boundary. The setting up of Christian villages in the southern part of Tamilnadu is illustrative of this particular understanding of boundary — boundary as a fence. For example, Mudalur (meaning, First Town) in South Tamilnadu came into existence as a Christian village at the beginning of the nineteenth century precisely to separate and protect new converts from their former Hindu neighbors.

3. Boundaries are "frontiers from which to venture out into new horizons to expand one's knowledge and one's circle of relationships."[19] Experiencing boundary as a frontier is possible only in the instance of actually crossing one's boundaries. In the *process* of crossing the boundary, one finds oneself in a frontier situation. New horizons open up, and one's knowledge of the other and the world expands. In my introduction to South Indian classical music, I literally saw new horizons open up before me. Furthermore, one's circle of relationships widens far beyond one's imagination. My crossing of religious boundaries has widened my circle of friends, which now includes Hindus, Muslims, Buddhists, Jews, and Sikhs on the one hand, and people of various nations and languages on the other. The theological practice that emerges in our crossing of boundaries is that which assists us "in transcending differences of all kinds and opening up new frontiers to build a 'civilization of love,' which is not merely a confirmation of old identities but a forging of a new, common identity in which the worst of each group is overcome and the best is combined to produce truly intercultural human beings in the image of the triune God."[20]

In all these various manifestations of boundaries and the crossing of them, one can detect flashes of relativization. The very boundaries that define us, direct us, and defend us are relativized. One is led to question and to reformulate one's definitions of self and the other, one's view of community, and one's aesthetic imagination. Such relativization can happen and does happen as a result of one's faith in God. When God is adored as God — the ultimate point of reference for our lives in this world — all else is relativized. A theological practice such as this generates a lot of tension. As Gordon Kaufman writes,

Faith in God, if God is taken seriously as the ultimate point of reference in terms of which all else is to be understood and relativized, means living with a certain tension in all our moral and intellectual convictions and judgments, a tension demanding that we always take into account the questionableness and thus the necessity to revise, correct, and refine them. It is a tension that must leave us always unsatisfied with our own insights and understanding, a tension always urging us to reach beyond our present position.[21]

Living with these tensions is truly a theological practice. It is within this tension that we find our integrity and our freedom. As Kaufman writes elsewhere:

If the self is to gain its own integrity and become truly free, all finite attachments must be restricted and delimited by the self's loyalty and devotion to that highest reality which is above and behind and under them all. Attachment to God, through relativizing all other attachments, can free the self from idolatrous bondage to them.[22]

Our contemporary world greatly suffers from destructive loyalties to that which is not God. Our involvement in violence and war, our indifference to poverty and oppression, and our unending thirst for consumption are all reflections of our idolatrous allegiances to the penulimates, forsaking the only ultimate, God. Yet at the same time, our period is rampant with opportunities and possibilities to cross every boundary that separates us from one another. The processes of globalization have compressed our world in such a way that boundaries are crossed every second in today's world. Therefore, we need to awaken to the possibility and desirability of boundary-crossing as a theological practice, which in turn will lead us all to make real the dictum: Let God be God!

Notes

1. Timothy Gorringe, *Karl Barth: Against Hegemony* (Oxford: Oxford University Press, 1999).

2. Ibid., 5.

3. H. Richard Niebuhr, *The Purpose of the Church and Its Ministry* (New York: Harper & Row, 1956), 39.

4. Ibid., 46.

5. Gordon D. Kaufman, *The Theological Imagination: Constructing the Concept of God* (Philadelphia: Westminster Press, 1981), 269.

6. The Church of South India came into existence in 1947 as an organic union of Anglican, Presbyterian, Methodist, and Congregationalist churches in South India.

7. Some of the observations here belong to a particular period in the 1950s in South Tamilnadu. Today the situation with regard to gender relations is dramatically different.

8. This idea results from the practice of commensality within the Indian caste system.

9. Martin M. C. Yang, "How a Chinese Village Was Written," in *Crossing Cultural Boundaries: The Anthropological Experience,* ed. Solon T. Kimball and James B. Watson (San Francisco: Chandler Publishing Company, 1972), 73.

10. Saivites are those Hindus who name the Ultimate Reality (God) as Shiva.

11. Anthony Gittins, *Gifts and Strangers: Meeting the Challenge of Inculturation* (New York: Paulist Press, 1989), 132.

12. For an excellent discussion of the variety of "salvations," see Mark Heim, *Salvations: Truth and Difference in Religion* (Maryknoll, NY: Orbis Books, 1995).

13. Saint Anselm, *Basic Writings: Proslogium, Monologium, Gaunilon's On Behalf of the Fool, Cur Deus Homo,* trans. S. N. Deane, with an introduction by Charles Hartshone (La Salle, IL: Open Court, 1962).

14. Gordon D. Kaufman, *In Face of Mystery: A Constructive Theology* (Cambridge, MA: Harvard University Press, 1993), 67.

15. Don Saliers and Emily Saliers, *A Song to Sing, a Life to Live: Reflections on Music as Spiritual Practice* (San Francisco: Jossey-Bass, 2005), xvi.

16. Ibid., 181.

17. Peter C. Phan, *In Our Own Tongues: Perspectives from Asia on Mission and Inculturation* (Maryknoll, NY: Orbis Books, 2003), 137.

18. Ibid.

19. Ibid.

20. Ibid.

21. Kaufman, *In Face of Mystery,* 8.

22. Kaufman, *The Theological Imagination,* 74–75.

6

A THEOLOGY OF
BORDER PASSAGE

KWOK PUI-LAN

I feel I exist on the boundaries...
somewhere between science and art, art and architecture...
public and private, east and west....
I am always trying to find a balance between these opposing
    forces...
finding the place where opposites meet...
existing not on either side, but on the line that divides...
and that line takes on a dimensionality; it takes on a sense of place
    and shape....   — Maya Lin, *Boundaries*[1]

Maya Lin, a renowned architect and artist, created public art to memorialize the Vietnam War veterans, the civil rights movement, and the
women in Yale University, as well as other public and private artworks.
Born to Chinese immigrant parents, Lin grew up in Ohio and started
making things in her father's art studio when she was very young.
Her monuments allow viewers to capture the architectonic memory of
complex and shifting historical events in private ways, in public space.
Whether it is water gushing out of stone, glass flowing like water, or the
inscription of names on black granite, her art, in her own words, "seek[s]
to create an intimate dialogue with the viewer, to allow a place of con-
templation, sometimes an incorporation of history, always a reliance on
time, memory, a passage or journey."[2]

In this essay, I want to explore the "sense of place and shape" of
border passage[3] and the implications for theological reflection in the

twenty-first century. I prefer to use "border passage" instead of "border crossing" to indicate that it is a continuous journey and not a fait accompli. Border passage is an important part of modern and collective history, which impacts the private lives of individuals in intimate ways. The border may be physical and geographical, as millions have left their country of origin to become immigrants, refugees, expatriates, diasporans, and people in exile. The border may be cultural, linguistic, and political, as Gloria Anzaldúa has powerfully articulated in her book *Borderlands*.[4] The border may be religious and civilizational, conjured as the "Islamic world," "Hindu civilization," or "East-Asian culture." The border has been mapped out frequently in terms of the body and body politic, topics that preoccupy queer theorists and other avant-garde critics. The border may also be imaginary, when we play with the notions of the "in-between space," the "third space," the "imaginary homeland," and other similar constructs.

In our globalized world in which time and space seem to have shrunk, many have argued that traditional borders do not hold anymore, as the market economy and the information highway have linked so many people together in unprecedented ways. Thomas L. Friedman, a *New York Times* columnist, has argued that "the world is flat" because of the lowering of trade and political barriers and the instantaneous speed with which we can connect to billions of other people in doing business, sharing ideas and information, and creating culture and knowledge.[5] Others, however, do not share Friedman's optimism of such a brave new world. Samuel P. Huntington's theory of the clash of civilizations has gained fervent followers, especially after September 11, 2001. He has argued that after the Cold War the threat of violence is no longer defined by ideologies, but by the clash of civilizations.[6] His view of civilizations as bound and separated from each other has been disparaged by critics as essentialist and outdated. In the redrawing of borders and the complex reconstituting of identities, genders, boundaries, nationalities, and ethnicities, what can scholars of religion and theologians of Asian descent who have for various reasons crisscrossed multiple sociocultural boundaries contribute to the conversation?

The Root and Route of Theologies in Asia

Asian theologies have never been stable and always border on two or more cultural worlds: the Middle East meets the East, Anselm encounters

Confucius, Jesus greets the Korean *minjung* or the Indian subaltern, the Syro-Phoenecian woman meets her sisters clad in saris or sarongs. As a cultural form, theologies in Asia have been [*hybrids*] from the beginning, since Christian ideas, symbols, and thought forms had to be rearticulated by other languages, cultural idioms, and thought patterns. In China, for example, when the Nestorian missionaries from Syria arrived at the Chinese court in the seventh century, they used largely Buddhist and Taoist terminologies and concepts to express Christian faith. The inscriptions on the famous Nestorian tablet are in Chinese with Syriac on the borders. The Nestorian cross arose out of a lotus and clouds surrounded by dragons. Centuries later, Matteo Ricci (1552–1610) learned the Chinese language, called himself "Western Confucian," and believed that Christianity had to adapt to Chinese culture to take root. Ricci's religious writings sought to combine Christian teachings with Confucian ethics and values.

Such openness to indigenous cultures changed drastically during the age of colonialism, when the missionary enterprise colluded with state power and military might. R. S. Sugirtharajah has shown that, during this period, the Bible assumed the status of a tangible signifier for white colonial cultures: "From now on, it will be distributed throughout the world as an icon containing civilizing properties."[7] The uplifting of the heathen foreigners became the irresistible "white man's burden." Asian cultures and religions were castigated as superstitious, backward, and idolatrous. Reflecting on the missionary legacy, Korean theologian Yong Bock Kim writes:

> The heritages of the Asian peoples were regarded as discontinuous with the gospel, from the Western Christian point of view, and therefore they did not have any positive place in theological reflection. Paganization of the gospel and syncretism of theology were much feared, in favor of the westernized gospel. In spite of such "theological containment" practiced against Asian heritages, the "native" Christian life was inevitably mingled with the religions and cultures of the peoples in Asia.[8]

After the 1960s, when most of the Asian countries regained political independence, the urgent theological question was how theologies in Asia could break out of this "theological containment." The indigenization of the gospel into Asian soil became crucial if the Asian churches were to rid themselves of the colonial legacy. During the period of nation building, Indian theologian M. M. Thomas argued that Christianity was relevant to the Asian struggles because the gospel transcends all cultures and should not be identified with Western culture and Western imperialism.[9] He further redefined the task of theology in his context: "Indian Christian theology is understood here as reflections in an articulated form on God, Christ and the Church at the point of the meeting of the Christian faith with Indian people and their world-views, cultures and beliefs."[10] Thomas's pioneering work sought to reconnect Christian theology with the sociopolitical and religiocultural contexts of Asia, and to liberate the gospel from the straitjacket imposed by the West.

Two theologians instrumental in rerouting Asian theologies are Choanseng Song from Taiwan and Aloysius Pieris from Sri Lanka. Song argues that the journey from Israel to Asia must be undertaken all over again. In the past, the trip was predetermined in the West and needed to make too many intermediary stopovers, with too many attractions and interruptions. The passengers spent too much time visiting Gothic churches and cathedrals and consulting with learned scholars of Western Christianity, to the extent that they have come dangerously close to "disowning [their] own cultural heritage as having no useful meaning in the design of God's salvation."[11] To remedy this, Song insists that the journey must make fewer stops and allow changes of itinerary or rerouting when occasions demand. And the passengers must work out the itinerary themselves, instead of relying on others.

 Song uses the term "transposition" to describe this journey from Israel to Asia. Transposition means a shift of time and space. For him, Christian faith was transposed from Palestine to the Greco-Roman world, and eventually to the West. Although it has been transposed to Asia and other parts of the Third World by the missionary movements, they have not taken root because Christianity has not "become flesh" in the native cultures. Transposition is not simply a translation into another language, style, or expression, but requires "theological discussion to shift to different subjects, to face new questions, and to discover alternative approaches."[12] Song's theological hybrids use stories from many Asian societies, ancient and modern, to illuminate and uncover the meaning of the biblical tradition.

Through his writings and his leadership role in the Program for Theology and Cultures in Asia, Song has inspired a generation of Asian theologians to recover their own cultural and spiritual resources for doing living theologies in Asia. His work has facilitated the development of story theology in Asia, along with cross-textual hermeneutics and creative indigenous approaches to theology. It supports and guides Asian Christians in the border passage of rediscovery of their cultural roots after a long period of colonialism. Yet his approach is not without drawbacks. First, coming from a Reformed tradition, Song's theology is very Bible-centered. His biblical interpretation is rather traditional, drawing primarily from mainline male scholars and paying little attention to newer methods. He is more reluctant than other Asian theologians, especially the feminists among them, in critiquing the biblical texts. Second, though Song has very open and inclusive attitudes toward people's cultures and stories, his theology remains very christocentric. While he uses Asian stories and resources to retell the Jesus story, the essential features of the plot remain somewhat unchanged. Third, scholars have questioned whether Song has created a binary between Asia and the West and whether the anti-colonial rhetoric is still useful today. I shall return to this criticism momentarily.

If Song's theological hybrids accent symbols, stories, and people's movements, Aloysius Pieris highlights Asian religiosities and spiritualities. As a Jesuit, Pieris argues that the Western models of inculturation are not suitable for Asia. The Latin model of "incarnation in a non-Christian *culture*," and the Greek model of "assimilation of a non-Christian *philosophy*" are least applicable in contemporary Asia. Instead, he advocates the monastic model, which is the "participation in a non-Christian *spirituality*."[13] For too long, Christianity has adopted the attitude of a "Christ-against-religions." The inculturists have advocated a "Christ-of-religions," but have often separated religion from liberation struggles.[14] A Third World theology of religions, for Pieris, must link spirituality with the liberation of people from poverty.

Pieris has always spoken out from the border of Christianity and Buddhism, which he has studied very closely. He has been criticized for generalizing religion and poverty as the two distinctive characteristics of the Asian continent and for flattening many differences. He tends to make very broad generalizations for his theological schema and typologies, which can be misleading at times. For example, his differentiation of Asian religiousness as cosmic and metacosmic may not do justice to the vast varieties and nuances of Asian traditions and practices. His broad generalization that Western religiosity is agapeic and Eastern religiosity is gnostic,[15] though helpful in a certain sense, does not pay sufficient attention to the differences within Asian traditions, for example, between Confucianism and Buddhism, and the enormous diversities within each of the traditions. His opting for a monastic paradigm may also reinforce the colonial stereotypes of the mythic, passive, religious "East" versus a progressive, active, and secular "West."[16]

M. M. Thomas, Choan-seng Song, and Aloysius Pieris emerged on the Asian theological scene when many Asian countries were poor and struggling for cultural affirmation. Today, when the economic and political situations of Asian societies have rapidly changed, especially among those on the so-called Pacific Rim, what kind of Asian theologies will be able to speak to this new situation? Do we need another rerouting for our time? Will the kinds of *minjung* theology, homeland theology, and the theology of struggle proposed during an earlier period be able to offer continued guidance, or do we need something else?

In the rerouting of theologies in our current contexts, we must pay attention to how the forces of globalization are reshaping the history and peoples of the Asia-Pacific. Hong Kong, for example, has grown from a relatively poor city in the 1970s to become one of the world's major financial centers and a critical link in the global market. With economic growth and market expansion, Asians have retrieved "Asian values" in order to argue for an "Asian" way of modernization and development. From Tokyo to Singapore, Neo-Confucianism has been valorized as performing the equivalent functions of Calvinism during an earlier time, when capitalism developed in Europe. In India, Hinduism has been touted as the essence of the Indian people, disregarding the heritages of the minorities and indigenous groups. Muslim fundamentalism has been revitalized in various parts of Asia. If we had to recover from a loss of cultural confidence after the colonial period, Asian politicians and cultural pundits today are busy proclaiming that our communalism, relational ethics, and group mentality are much better than Western individualism. In the rehashing of "Asian values," the patriarchal biases are left intact and, even worse, they can be used to reinforce the "family value" discourse of the neo-conservatives in America in their support of global capitalism.

It is at this historical juncture that the body of work by Sugirtharajah is significant. Born and raised in Sri Lanka and having developed his postcolonial thinking at Birmingham, where cultural studies began as an academic discipline, Sugirtharajah is an astute commentator of the "hermeneutical odyssey" that Asian theologians and biblical critics have taken.[17] He brings us back to the precolonial time, when the Bible interacted with Asian cultures as one of the many religious texts. He delineates the colonial tools and shows that Asian scholars are not free from the Anglicized or self-Orientalizing modes of interpretation. He articulates a "hermeneutics in transit" to facilitate postcolonial and diasporic border passages that many Asian intellectuals have embarked on:

> Postcoloniality is perhaps the sign of an increased realization that it is not feasible to deduct a civilization, a custom, a narrative history, a literature, from the wider influences and trends of the increasingly shrinking globalized world. In other words, it is not always feasible to recover one's authentic "roots" or even to go back to the real "home" again.... The Third World as a whole is marked by diversity rather than homogeneity.... The interpreter, whether diasporic or indigenous, achieves originality and autonomy not by jettisoning native impulses or by uncritically embracing metropolitan values, but ... by working through them.[18]

The Odyssey of Border Intellectuals and Theologians

What does it entail to do theology when one is situated between several cultures and groups or when one occupies the interstices of the local and the global and has multiple belongings and loyalties? More than ever, the familiar and comfortable markers of our identities and the vantage points from where we used to speak have been called into question, especially by the younger generation of scholars. Nami Kim, a Korean theologian teaching in the United States, has challenged the uncritical use of the unifying category of "Asia" and traced its roots back to a Japanese colonial impulse in creating Pan-Asianism and the Greater East Asian Co-prosperity Sphere. The Koreans were colonized by the Japanese. Kim uses the narrative of comfort women during the Second World War to complicate the postcolonial discourse, which has hitherto focused on "Asia" and the "West." She does not believe that "Asian" feminist theologians should reverse their gaze from the "Western" global to the "Asian" local. Instead she wants to reroute "Asian" feminist theology so that it will be a critical global feminist theology, for which "Asian" is an "imagined community" and not determined by country of origin or through racial/ethnic affiliation.[19]

Writing from Hong Kong, Wai-Ching Angela Wong has emerged as an important voice for her critique of the construction of the "Asian poor woman" in the earlier phases of Asian feminist theologies.[20] She finds Song's cultural hybrids outdated and the early generation of Asian feminist theologians' theological constructs confining, and sets out to create her own. If Kosuke Koyama had conjured waterbuffalo theology, based on his imagination of a rural Asia,[21] Wong is determined to evoke the sensibilities of city-dwellers. Based on the tales spun in the cosmopolitan city of Hong Kong, Wong questions the binary construction of the "East" and the "West" and the suffering-liberation script of Asian feminist theology. Along the way, she enlists the help of French poststructuralist theories to unpack the formation of subject-in-process. Wong does not resist story theology; she simply does not like the stories told by an earlier generation and proceeds to find newer narratives. It is premature to predict what shapes Asian theologies will take in the future, when the "natives" can no longer be imagined as outside the globalized circuits, but are increasingly occupying a strategic and influential part in it.

What happens when the usual signage in our border passage becomes more blurred, and the banner under which we have done our theology becomes less clear than before? What happens to the psychic life of border intellectuals and theologians when they are taking this journey that is both public and private? How does one negotiate an identity that seems elusive and hard to grasp — that when you feel you have finally found an anchor, you need to search all over again? How does a theologian live with a haunted history — disjointed, constantly shifting, and refusing to be fitted into one piece? To use Maya Lin's words, how does one live on that line, "which takes on a dimensionality?"

Maya Lin was only a college senior when she won the competition for the design of the Vietnam Veterans Memorial. After studying many public memorials and monuments, she has designed the memorial following one simple impulse: "to cut into the earth." As she writes, "I imagined taking a knife and cutting into the earth, opening it up, an initial violence and pain that in time would heal."[22] That her simple design accompanied by a hand-written description became the winner of the competition was serendipitous. The much-acclaimed memorial, with fifty-seven thousand names of the fallen soldiers in chronological order from 1959 to 1975, is a site of collective memory of the scar that has been left. The shining surface of the granite is a boundary that separates the living from the world of the dead, to which persons with these names have gone. In front of this very public memorial, viewers can find a space for private grieving. No one, on seeing the relatives and friends touching or rubbing the names of the departed ones, cannot feel a heavy sense of history and the human cost.

Like the Vietnam Veterans Memorial, the work of the border theologians evokes the burden of history, and for them it is the experience of dislocation and displacement. They bear witness to the trauma, grief, and injuries that typically accompany "border-crossing," whose lingering effects continue to plague their communities and leave a long-lasting scar. Andrew Sung Park uses the term *"han*-ridden community" to describe the Korean community caught in the racial conflict with African Americans in the struggle to survive in a dominant white society.[23] This *han* has not gone away but has taken a different shape within generations of Asian American communities who have a long history in America. Gale A. Yee, a third-generation Chinese American biblical scholar, speaks of the "coercive mimeticism" in which she is repeatedly asked to perform cultural scripts of a racial/ethnic person assigned by the dominant society, and in so doing to authenticate their preconceptions.[24] Frank M. Yamada, a sansei (third-generation) Japanese American scholar recounts the effects of the imposed silence on the generation that has gone to the internment camps during the Second World War and the need to demonstrate that they are doubly American.[25]

Some of the most famous border intellectuals have turned to psychoanalytical theories for language to describe their trauma, grief, alienation, and melancholy: Frantz Fanon on the angst of the black man, Julia Kristeva on the mourning of the maternal body, Homi Bhabha on colonial mimicry, and Judith Butler on queer life. I have been generally skeptical of psychoanalysis, because of its universalizing tendencies and its rather narrow focus on familial narratives. However, the works of scholars who have subjected psychoanalysis to a postcolonial or racialized reading with critical acumen have expanded my view. They have shown that Freud's psychoanalysis must be read together with the colonial European context[26] and that the psychoanalytical language offers insight to unpack the racialized, hyphenated, or fractured identity that border theologians have been talking about.

If border theology is not just to celebrate the wonders of heteroglossia, the carnival of differences, and the joy of arrival, it must attend to the complicated, conflicting, and interlocking emotions of grief, loss, and wounding in our psychical drama, the kind of "desire and doubt, affirmation and rejection, projection and identification, management and dysfunction" that Anne Anlin Cheng has described with vivid details.[27] In a much-quoted passage, Japanese American theologian Fumitaka Matsuoka describes the experience of "in-between" two worlds:

> A liminal world is the "place of in-betweenness." It is at once the world of isolation and intimacy, desolation and creativity. A person in a liminal world is poised in uncertainty and ambiguity between two or more social constructs, reflecting in the soul the discords and harmonies, repulsions and attractions. One of the constructs is likely to be dominant, whether cultural or linguistic. Within such a dominant construct one strives to belong and yet finds oneself to be a peripheral member, forced to remain in the world of in-betweenness.[28]

Before we rush to distill from this the themes of liminality or marginality in Asian American identity and theology, it is important to pause and pay attention to the searing words of "isolation and intimacy, desolation and creativity... uncertainty and ambiguity... discords and harmonies, repulsions and attractions," and ask what exactly do these words memorialize.

For Cheng, such physical drama memorializes the racial grief in the identity formation of the racialized subject: "To see racial identity as a melancholic formation is to apprehend that identity's instability and its indebtedness to the dis-identity it is also claiming."[29] Matsuoka describes the wounding memories of both love and hate when he wants to belong, but is left on the periphery. This dis-identification constitutes a separation, a loss that is permanently located in the deep layers of the psyche. I want to suggest that this double take of identification and dis-identification is experienced not only by racialized subjects, but also increasingly by people who find their cultures and ways of life impinged upon by the globalized culture and capitalist consumerism.

I suggest that it is the tensions, contradictions, and fragments that characterize the border subject. It is more complicated than the sinner and the sinned-against, the *han*-ridden and the *han*-exorcised paradigms articulated in theological anthropologies from an earlier period. It requires the description of the subject not as hero or villain, but as a much more complex, three-dimensional subject situated in the enthralling plots of irony, between satire and despair, between rage and empathy, between absurdity and hopefulness.

A Border Theology of "Not Quite"

In *Powers of Horror,* Julia Kristeva has developed the theory of abjection, in which the abject is expelled and pushed to the boundary of the self. For her the abjection of the self is based on "the inaugural *loss* that laid the foundations of its own being."[30] In her psychoanalytical theory, that inaugural *loss* is the loss of the maternal body, the semiotics, when one enters the symbolic, the Law of the father. But if we read her theory in terms of her border passage from Bulgaria to metropolitan Paris, we can see the grieving for her, for the maternal body also means the loss of the mother language, culture, and the kind of Christianity with which she was familiar.[31]

On the complex notion of the abjection of the self, Kristeva writes:

If it be true that the abject simultaneously beseeches and pulverizes the subject, one can understand that it is experienced at the peak of its strength when that subject, weary of fruitless attempts to identify with something on the outside, finds the impossible within, when it finds that the impossible constitutes its very *being*, that it is none other than abject.[32]

A border theology must address this "impossible within," which constitutes the love and hate drama of "isolation and intimacy . . . desolation and creativity, repulsions and attractions." I would like to suggest a theology of "not quite" to articulate the grief, loss, and tensions of the border subject. Postcolonial theorist Homi Bhabha identifies the grief of the colonial mimicry as "almost the same, *but not quite.*"[33] Anne Anlin Cheng describes the grief of a racialized subject as "assimilating, but not quite," because they are racially different. Asian Americans are not quite "Asian" and not quite "American." And increasingly, even the

Asians who are not in diaspora do not know if they are quite "Asian" anymore, and for some, there is a flight from being "Asian" — the very popular dyeing of hair to look "white" among young Asian women in metropolitan cities is a salient example.

But the horizon of the "not quite" opens a new dimensionality of thinking about God. (God is that which cannot be fully grasped by our language and bound by our experiences and fantasies. God always exists outside any totalitarian effort and resists any attempt of full narration. It is because no revelation can be a full disclosure that allows new and ingenious narratives to be narrated.)

A theology of "not quite" has a dimensionality of time. In the gospel narratives Jesus repeatedly said that his time has not come yet. And when the time comes, we will fully know him and the truths that he fully embodies. The Jewish people living under the Roman Empire had the messianic hope of another time that was not yoked to imperial time. And it was the expectation of "not yet" that became the symbolization of their hope.

This theology also has a dimensionality of spatiality, which resists any totalitarian occupation or homogenization. One of the most important symbols is when Jesus laments for Jerusalem and says that he wishes to protect the city of peace, like the mother hen protecting her brood. Even the stones in Palestine bear witness to the irony and tragedy of history as if they would cry out at any time. After the death of Jesus, when all hope seems to have collapsed and the horizon closed, the women found the empty tomb. They could not find the body there. With the empty tomb, the Christians constructed their memory and spun a new tale. It is a story that is not finished, a body that is not fixed, and a story that resists final closure.

Theology is always about time and space, for theology has been so much tied to the history and destiny of a people: the Israelites, the story of the early Christians, and the church as the people of God. But theology has a very dialectical understanding of time and space. The Hebrew people recalled that "a wandering Aramean was our ancestor." The story of the exodus people, going through the journey in the wilderness, became their paradigmatic story. The prophets evoked that story again and again whenever they had become complacent and satisfied, and wanted to create nations, temples, and rituals for settling down. Journey, passage, and crossing always relativize and disrupt space, whether it is the

...ation, or the temple. In recalling the journey and re-
...ir rituals, the past and the present become one, and the
... once again called into responsibility. The fact that they
...ie on the journey becomes the foundation for providing
...s who are strangers, aliens, and immigrants.

...has never been fully incorporated into world history
...of God and the city of humans are always in tension with
one another. The true invisible church is always at odds with the church
that wields so much power and cooperates with the crown. Throughout
the ages, the pilgrims and the monks who have gone out to the desert to
form communities on the border and other alternative base communities
have created important sites of resistance and renewal.

The time and space of "not quite" is not easy to inhabit, for it is
internally transgressive. It troubles the national, racial, ethnic, class,
gendering, and ecclesial tales that homogenize difference, suppress the
minorities, and coerce everyone to be the same. It is the expungation
of the "not quite" that undergirds the violent and uncompromising religious and ethnic strife that we have witnessed since the end of the
so-called Cold War. It is not the clash of "civilizations" that we are wit-
nessing, but the clash "within."[34] It is the abjection of the "not quite"
that best explains the Vatican's silencing of dissident theologians and the
churches' pushing away of unwanted and queer bodies.

A theology of border passage is transgressive for it defiles the whole,
resists assimilation, and resolutely stands on the border of the holy. It
refuses to accept doctrinal purity based on the power of one tale, and
it welcomes many narratives. It democratizes the sacred by locating the
holy in many cultures, practices, and multiple stories. It remembers the
lost innocence and the martyrs who have gone to the other side, lives
sacrificed for the sake of "noble" causes, national tales, and narratives
of empire, in any given time and any space.

Notes

1. Maya Lin, *Boundaries* (New York: Simon & Schuster, 2000). I have shaped
these lines, which appeared as fragments in the original text, into a poem.

2. Ibid., 2:03.

3. The term "border passage" is inspired by Leila Ahmed, *A Border Passage:
From Cairo to America — A Woman's Journey* (New York: Farrar, Straus, and
Giroux, 1999).

4. Gloria Anzaldúa, *Borderlands: The New Mestiza=La Frontera* (San Francisco: Spinsters/Aunt Lute, 1987).

5. Thomas L. Friedman, *The World Is Flat: A Brief History of the Twenty-First Century* (New York: Farrar, Straus and Giroux, 2005).

6. Samuel P. Huntington, *The Clash of Civilizations and the Remaking of World Order* (New York: Simon & Schuster, 1996).

7. R. S. Sugirtharajah, "Biblical Studies after the Empire: From a Colonial to a Postcolonial Mode of Interpretation," in *The Postcolonial Bible*, ed. Sugirtharajah (Sheffield: Sheffield Academic Press, 1998), 14–15. See also R. S. Sugirtharajah, *The Bible and the Third World: Precolonial, Colonial and Postcolonial Encounters* (Cambridge: Cambridge University Press, 2001).

8. Yong Bock Kim, "Doing Theology in Asia Today: A Korean Perspective," in *Asian Christian Theology: Emerging Themes*, ed. Douglas J. Elwood (Philadelphia: Westminster Press, 1980), 315–16.

9. M. M. Thomas, *The Christian Response to the Asian Revolution* (London: SCM Press, 1966).

10. M. M. Thomas, "Introduction" in M. M. Thomas and P. T. Thomas, *Towards an Indian Christian Theology: Life and Thought of Some Pioneers* (Tiruvalla: New Day Publications of India, 1992), 1. See also Sathianathan Clarke, "M. M. Thomas," in *Empire and the Christian Tradition: New Readings of Classical Theologians*, ed. Kwok Pui-lan, Don H. Compier, and Joerg Rieger (Minneapolis: Augsburg Fortress Press, forthcoming).

11. C. S. Song, *The Compassionate God* (Maryknoll, NY: Orbis Books, 1982), 7.

12. Ibid., 9.

13. Aloysius Pieris, *An Asian Theology of Liberation* (Maryknoll, NY: Orbis Books, 1988), 51.

14. Ibid., 88.

15. Ibid., 56. To Pieris's credit, he does say the agapeic and the gnostic are not mutually exclusive.

16. See Richard King, *Orientalism and Religion: Postcolonial Theory, India and the "Mythic East"* (London: Routledge, 1999).

17. R. S. Sugirtharajah, "Cultures, Texts, Margins: A Hermeneutical Odyssey," in his *Asian Biblical Hermeneutics and Postcolonialism* (Maryknoll, NY: Orbis Books, 1998), 123–39.

18. R. S. Sugirtharajah, "Hermeneutics in Transit," in his *Postcolonial Criticism and Biblical Interpretation* (Oxford: Oxford University Press, 2002), 197–98.

19. Nami Kim, " 'My/Our' Comfort *Not* at the Expense of 'Somebody Else's,' " *Journal of Feminist Studies in Religion* 21, no. 2 (2005): 75–94; and "The 'Indigestible' Asian: The Unifying Term 'Asian' in Theological Discourse," in *Off the Menu: Asian and Asian North American Women's Religion and Theology*, ed. Rita Nakashima Brock et al., (Louisville: Westminster John Knox Press, forthcoming).

20. Wai-Ching Angela Wong, *"The Poor Woman": A Critical Analysis of Asian Theology and Contemporary Chinese Fiction by Women* (New York: Peter Lang, 2002).

21. Kosuke Koyama, *Waterbuffalo Theology* (Maryknoll, NY: Orbis Books, 1974).

22. Lin, *Boundaries*, 4:10.

23. Andrew Sung Park, *Racial Conflict and Healing: An Asian-American Theological Perspective* (Maryknoll, NY: Orbis Books, 1996).

24. Gale A. Yee, "Yin/Yang Is Not Me: An Exploration into an Asian American Biblical Hermeneutics," in *Ways of Being, Ways of Reading: Asian American Biblical Interpretation,* ed. Mary F. Foskett and Jeffrey Kah-Jin Kuan (St. Louis: Chalice Press, 2006), 154.

25. Frank M. Yamada, "Constructing Hybridity and Heterogeneity: Asian American Biblical Interpretation from a Third-Generation Perspective," in *Ways of Being, Ways of Reading: Asian American Biblical Interpretation,* ed. Mary F. Foskett and Jeffrey Kah-Jin Kuan (St. Louis: Chalice Press, 2006), 171.

26. Ranjana Khanna, *Dark Continents: Psychoanalysis and Colonialism* (Durham, NC: Duke University Press, 2003).

27. Anne Anlin Cheng, *The Melancholy of Race: Psychoanalysis, Assimilation, and Hidden Grief* (New York: Oxford University Press, 2001), 15.

28. Fumitaka Matsuoka, *Out of Silence: Emerging Themes in Asian American Churches* (Cleveland: United Church Press, 1995), 54.

29. Cheng, *The Melancholy of Race,* 24.

30. Julia Kristeva, *Powers of Horror: An Essay on Abjection* (New York: Columbia University Press, 1982), 5. Emphasis hers. For a helpful discussion of Kristeva's theory in Korean American theology, see Wonhee Anne Joh, *Heart of the Cross: A Postcolonial Christology* (Louisville: Westminster John Knox Press, 2006).

31. Julia Kristeva, *Strangers to Ourselves* (New York: Columbia University Press, 1991).

32. Kristeva, *Powers of Horror,* 5.

33. Homi K. Bhabha, "Of Mimicry and Man: The Ambivalence of Colonial Discourse," in *The Location of Culture* (London: Routledge, 1994), 85–92.

34. Arjun Appadurai, *Fear of Small Numbers: An Essay on the Geography of Anger* (Durham, NC: Duke University Press, 2006).

PART THREE

PEDAGOGICAL PERSPECTIVES

7

CURRICULUM TRANSFORMATION

Dreaming of Decolonization
in Theological Studies

Musa W. Dube

*Scholars of biblical studies, or, for that matter, scholars working
in the field of theological studies have yet to address the relation
between European expansion and the rise of their own discipline.
More importantly, there is yet to be a theological critique of the
empire, especially among English theologians.*

— R. S. Sugirtharajah[1]

During the second presidential debate of 2004 in the United States, President George Bush was asked why he barred importing cheaper drugs from Canada. His response was that he wanted to "protect Americans" by making sure that they do not end up receiving drugs purporting to be from Canada but coming from the "Third World." Senator John Kerry countered this by saying that President Bush barred cheaper drugs from Canada because he wants to give the business to bigger companies in the United States.

My interest in President Bush's use of the "Third World" card to defend himself is not so much about its factuality. Rather, what interests me is what it indicates, what it draws upon, and its wider implications; namely, the historically based, thoroughly structural and institutionalized narrative representation of the Other, in this case, the so-called Third World. My interest is in the ideological boundaries of this representation, how it functions, and how it informs academic programs. I seek to examine the consequences of this particular representation of the Other, namely, *the structural exclusion of the Other through monitoring and working within particular ideological boundaries*. President Bush's claim/aim of protecting U.S. citizens from "Third World" drugs implies that the medical products are substandard, dangerous, and likely to hurt U.S. citizens; hence they are better barred. It does not take much to dispute the claim that dangerous medical drugs are solely from the "Third World."[2] If it were so, the drug companies in the United States would not be in the habit of pulling their drugs off the market because they have been found to cause health dangers, as happens, some would say, all too frequently. Similarly, medical establishments in the United States would not have suffered from numerous lawsuits, both for medical malpractice and drugs that have caused further injury to patients.

What then sustains George Bush's claim that he wanted to protect U.S. citizens from "Third World" drugs? What makes such a statement possible? Why is danger equated with the outside? President Bush is drawing upon historically, structurally, and institutionally embedded representations of the Other as underdeveloped and dangerous, hence worthy of exclusion. The dominant ideology has long established boundaries that legitimate exclusion and control inclusion. President Bush's "Third World" card depends on the colonial discourse of modern imperialism that has characterized the Other, their lands, products, cultures, religions, and philosophies as below standard, dangerous, exotic, childish, devilish, lazy, animalistic, and womanish. The Other represents all the negatives, which naturally are to be avoided. If the Other is included in any way, it must be done with great care and in controlled and non-threatening small doses.

Many authors have labored to document for us just how deeply entrenched this colonial discourse is.[3] They point out how colonialism has permeated everything, including academic paradigms. Many "othered" groups such as women, blacks, gays and lesbians, indigenous peoples, Jews, and the physically challenged have also documented how the Other has been constructed in the modern patriarchal Eurocentric view and for what purposes. Postcolonial studies, in particular, repeatedly demonstrate that academic disciplines such as history, anthropology, science, psychology, biology, English literature, film and the other arts, theology, and natural science were born and nourished in the modern colonial context. These disciplines have operated with a colonial discourse that has relegated the Other to the well-guarded ideological spaces of the "underdeveloped" or "developing" corner, spaces that the so-called developed nations can continue to oversee. In this well-established colonial discourse, the Others were named as "developing countries" or "underdeveloped nations." These terms, which tend to be normalized in day-to-day conversations, suggest that such areas are infants who must depend on the so-called "developed, First World" countries. Such terminology serves to legitimate the dominance of the so-called "First World" as the redeeming adults (Kipling). Thus it also sustains colonial discourse that holds that "development" must follow the path from Europe to Asia, Africa, and then to the ends of the world. Within these colonizing ideological boundaries, the Other was thus named as "Third World," a term that is commonly used when, in fact, these nations constitute the Two-Thirds World in both space and population. Therefore, the term "Third World" in itself ideologically allocates the Two-Thirds World masses to a much smaller space in the global economy. The term repeatedly inculcates in our minds that the Other constitutes just a small part of the world, only a third. It minimizes the presence and importance of the Other.

Such representations of the Other surface not only on the lips of a desperate president's attempt to retain power but also permeate most of our academic canons; most of our institutions, departments, and programs; most of our thinking, theories, methods, and philosophies. President Bush's use of the "Third World" card thus represents a larger historically and institutionally sustained colonial discourse, which includes even the guild of religious and theological studies. These ideologically defined and defended boundaries designate many as Other due to their gender, race, ethnicity, religion, nationality, sexuality, health, class, physical ability, or region. Be that as it may, since the last century the world has seen movements that struggle for liberation and justice from various fronts. Consequently, more often than not, people are likely to feel shy about standing up and being counted as overt supporters of racism, patriarchy, ethnic cleansing, apartheid, homophobia, colonialism, environmental degradation, and so on. For example, many academic institutions in the United States express their commitment to equality by striving to use politically correct language and subscribe to a policy of equal opportunity. Yet if the public picture is to show respect to all people through institutional policies of politically correct language and equal opportunity, does this stance translate into disavowing the use of a colonizing ideology in the academic programs and structures? It should.

Consequently, those who subscribe to teaching for liberating inter-dependence and transformation ought to continuously remain suspicious about how engulfed they are by, and most probably working within, the ideological boundaries of "developing" and "developed" nations, and how such boundaries serve as control valves for what is included and how it is included. Although champions of social transformation are indispensable to every struggle, teaching for liberating interdependence must go beyond the commitment and attempts by isolated individuals to programmatic transformation in theological studies. This calls for individual commitment, accountable solidarity, academic leadership and institutional commitment to curriculum transformation. It certainly calls for accountability that goes beyond the language of political correct-ness and equal opportunity policies; it must result in a commitment to curricular transformation that continuously interrogates how it in-habits the colonial and colonizing ideological space of the so-called "developed" and "developing." The use of "Third" and "First" worlds needs continuous interrogation by the academy. Academic theological and religious study programs need to suspiciously and continually in-terrogate how they might easily occupy these boundaries. In fact, R. S. Sugirtharajah points out that "scholars of biblical studies, or, for that matter scholars working in the field of theological studies have yet to address the relation between European expansionism and the rise of their own discipline.... Western theologians have yet to offer a sustained theological analysis of the impact of colonialism."[4]

I wish to contribute to this quest by sharing with you how I have been dreaming dreams of decolonization in my teaching and research and what I have discovered about myself and theological studies along the way. The quest of the essay is curriculum transformation in theological studies. I have chosen stories from five different institutions that I have interacted with to highlight how academic theological studies are in-scribed within colonizing academic boundaries. My hope is to stimulate dreams of others to decolonize the guild.

Briefly, the history of my theological education has found me in a number of different locations. I was at the University of Botswana (UB) first as a student (1984–88) and then as a faculty member (1992–2007).

During the latter period, I took time to do graduate studies at Durham and Vanderbilt Universities (1989–97), to work for the World Council of Churches (2002–3) as a gender and HIV&AIDS theological consultant; and to teach at Claremont Colleges, Scripps College (2004–5). I returned to the University of Botswana in 2005 and am currently based there. I want to share my encounter with colonial boundaries as a student, researcher, lecturer, and trainer of trainers in theological education and religious studies. My aim is to highlight how theological programs are often circumscribed by colonial boundaries and how curriculum transformation is needed in theological programs of the twenty-first century. The stories that I share here do not necessarily follow the chronological sequence of my theological journeys presented above.

Story 1: Designing and Teaching RLST 182: Methods of Biblical Interpretations

In the fall semester of 2004 when designing a new course on Methods of Biblical Interpretations, I began where I was "supposed" to begin: with the historical background of the Bible, followed by textual, source, traditional, redactional, compositional, and rhetorical criticisms. Then I proceeded to sociological and literary methods. This was followed by a second section that featured what I called the "Two-Thirds World Methods of Biblical Reading." Within this section I featured Latin American and Hispanic, Asian and Asian American, African and African American, Native American and Palestinian methods of reading and devoted a week (two sessions) to each area. The two sessions divided the time between the continental, diasporic, and feminist perspectives of each of these groups. The last part of my course outline featured feminist methods of biblical interpretations, which in fact referred to First World feminist readings since Two-Thirds World feminist readings were covered under their particular groups.

After completing my course outline I looked at it critically. When I read through the outline, I realized that I had begun with Eurocentric methods and in so doing I had placed the Two-Thirds World and feminist readings at the periphery. My syllabus was in fact endorsing and maintaining the Eurocentric views that represented the Other as its derivatives, located in its peripheries and oscillating around it. I decided to rewrite my course outline. I began the introduction with Fernando

Segovia's article, "And They Began to Speak in Other Tongues," where he categorizes methods of biblical interpretation into three methods: historical, sociocritical, and literary.[5] Segovia shows how the classical biblical methods of reading are implicated in colonial discourse, in silencing the Other by insisting on a universal and objective reading, which in fact meant interpreting the Bible from a Eurocentric perspective. I followed this introductory article with my own article on "Postcolonial Biblical Interpretations," where I tried to plot how methods of biblical interpretation are closely informed by the history of collaborating with, supporting, and maintaining the colonial discourse and ideology, or resisting and rejecting it.[6] With these two introductory articles, the course outline went on to explore methods of biblical interpretations in the Two-Thirds World. These featured the worlds and concerns of the Other, including interreligious experiences, liberation, race issues, globalization, decolonization, gender, and justice in general.

Finally, the semester began and we all began to speak in Other tongues, so to speak, or so I assumed! There was one Chinese-American student who had been in my Feminist Interpretations of the Bible class in the fall semester of 2004. After two weeks of class she came to me and said: "Why are we *not* applying these methods and theories of reading the Bible to biblical texts like we did in the feminist class last semester?" I pulled out my syllabus and said, "We are going to start applying these methods once we get to the section on historical critical methods, for it would be difficult for us to read according to methods of these particular groups!" She silently nodded in agreement. After she left, I spent considerable time reflecting on her question, my answer, and its implications. I had to admit that in as much as I had turned my course outline around, it was still very Eurocentric. By suggesting that the only methods that could be applied by all of us were the historical, sociological, and literary methods, I was implicitly subscribing to the claim of the Eurocentric methods to be objective, neutral, scientific, and universal. Applied correctly, these methods would supposedly lead all readers to bring out the same meaning from the text.[7] This experience of designing and teaching my own course was an interesting discovery.

One month after the semester started, we were through with our Two-Thirds World exploration and we moved to the section on historical critical, sociocritical, and literary methods. When I rechecked the First

World methods on biblical interpretations, I realized that they occupied two whole months of classes! Western feminist methods occupied the last week of the semester. This in itself was revealing, for the Two-Thirds World methods had perfectly occupied that one-third space in the course outline.

One aspect of representing the concerns of the Other not only *where* they appear in the story and what they do, but also *how much space* is allocated to them.[8] Often the amount of space allocated to the Other speaks for itself. It attests to the discourse of keeping the so-called under-developed and dangerous "Third World" out, as President Bush openly said. The small amount of space allocated to the Other consistently suggests that what the Two-Thirds World offers is not up to the standard of quality (a quality measured only according to the so-called "First World"). Given its "underdevelopment," it is not necessary to place the Other in the foreground. Such ideological inclusions of the Other do allow for non-threatening "tourist" inclusions as long as the big chunk, the focus, and the core remain Eurocentric.

The underlying ideological boundaries of the "Third World" card thus call for a much bolder, more deliberate crossing of established borders within the academy. How often they make us remain in that land called Eurocentrism, where the Other is supposed to oscillate around its periphery? As you can imagine, the next time I offer the course on biblical interpretation, I will further interrogate the prevailing colonial borders of the discourse and how they can be crossed.

Story 2: My Work as a New Testament Scholar

My second story is about how I have been interrogating the representations of the Other in the New Testament mission stories and how Western feminist readers have been interpreting mission stories. In particular, I have investigated feminist reclamation/reconstruction projects that have dealt with the representations of the Other in these mission/contact stories and how they deal with the power relations advanced by these stories.[9] Some of the stories I have looked at include the Canaanite woman in Matthew 21:15–28, a woman who went to meet Jesus on behalf of her severely demon-possessed daughter; the Samaritan woman by the well[10] and the so-called great commission in Matthew 28:18–20.

My interest has been in interrogating how the Other is represented in mission stories and how the experience of Christianity functioned compatibly with modern colonialism. I wanted to know why readers of the Bible in colonial times did not find it ethically problematic to collaborate with the colonial agents of their time. This led me to ask how the mission stories represent the Other and their lands. Given that Christianity functioned hand in glove with the modern imperialism of the mother countries, my questions were: How do mission stories present crossing borders? Do such stories make room for liberating interdependence and mutual exchange, or do they propound an ideology of suppression and domination? I wanted to know if Western feminist biblical readers took this context into account in the liberationist reading of the mission stories. In my explorations I found that the feminist biblical project has been too quick to highlight the role of biblical women and their history in the spread of the early church. Consequently, the ideology of subjugating the Other was often bracketed as feminist readers sought to take the crown away from Paul as the apostle church founder and to place it in the hands of the Canaanite woman.

While I acknowledge that there are and will always be multiple readings of each of these biblical stories, it is important to highlight the ideology that produces, sanctions, and maintains the Other as Other. The first two stories tend to characterize the Other as women of a particular reputation or questionable standing. For example, the Canaanite woman has a daughter who is severely demon-possessed. She desperately needs help, but she is ignored and labeled a dog. She finally gets help when she assures Jesus that she is content to pick up crumbs from under the table as would a dog.[11] Such an ideology authorizes or legitimates the domination of the Other by dehumanizing the woman. It resorts to a style of characterizing the Other as a woman who needs help, one who is evil and dangerous. It maintains boundaries by continuously making efforts to convince the Other to remain in her designated lowly space. Thus while the Other is never totally excluded from the colonizer's space, she is included only insofar as she knows and accepts that her place is under the table; her status is that of a dog; and her share is that of picking up crumbs. Rather than sitting at the main table and eating the bread as a full member of the family, hers is a "Third World" space.

One finds a similar ideology in the case of the Samaritan woman (John 4).[12] She is not just a woman but a Samaritan woman. Moreover, she is a Samaritan woman who has had five husbands or men, and is currently living with a man/husband who is not her own (v. 18). In their conversation, Jesus belittles the importance of her heritage and ancestors (vv. 11–21). He says he can give the Samaritan woman water that will quench her thirst permanently and lead her to eternal life (vv. 11–15). As a new well of living water, Jesus displaces Jacob's well (v. 13). Jesus also tells her that neither the Jews nor Samaritans would worship in their holy places, for God is spirit and those who worship God will worship in Spirit and Truth (vv. 23–24). Finally, Jesus is welcomed into Samaria as the "savior of the world" (v. 41), a title used for the Roman emperors.[13]

The story represents the Other of Samaria in the female gender, which in itself suggests subjugation. By characterizing her as having many husbands/men, it implies that she is possibly immoral and thus in need of salvation. Even more important, she can continue on this same path. The story belittles the importance of her ancestors and their achievements, and openly suggests a superior replacement. It also dismisses and belittles the worship places of the Other and positions Jesus as superior to all.

Even though Jesus has spoken negatively about her ancestors and religion, the Other represented by the Samarian woman supposedly still loves and welcomes her dominator, the savior of the world. Jesus is invited to come and stay with them. Jesus thus becomes a new and, presumably, a legitimate husband of Samaria. But this new relationship of Jesus with Samaritans is not new at all: it firmly occupies the boundaries, where the Other is safely relegated to the space of inferior and subordinate. This story challenges us to interrogate how Christian mission has been imagined and practiced in the past and present and how this reflects international relations in general. It also challenges us to interrogate how our theological programs, theories, research, and pedagogical practice occupy these colonizing ideological boundaries of the dangerous, inferior, and "developing" Third World space.

As I have argued elsewhere, the great commission encodes similar power relations in its representations of the Other.[14] The disciples are supposedly given power by the resurrected Jesus to go into the world and make disciples of all nations. But when we read the word of the resurrected Christ he says, "*All* authority in heaven and on earth has been given to me. Go therefore and make disciples of *all* nations . . . teaching them to *obey everything* that I have commanded you." A Christ who has all authority over heaven and earth is not only similar to the one in John's Gospel (construed as "the savior of the world") but is even far above him. The fact that people of the world must be taught to *obey everything* that Jesus taught indicates that the Christian mission assumes that the Other will be an "infant" or a student in the traditional sense. It suggests that the Christian disciple will teach and baptize the Other, who is a blank, an undeveloped slate. It does not suggest or make room for the Christian disciples to come with a spirit of mutual exchange and respect or in a posture suggested by Kwok Pui-lan of asking, "What treasures do you have to share?"[15] Kwok Pui-lan calls for a different ideology of crossing boundaries, different terms of encounter with the Other, and different terms of inclusion. The latter approach does not assume that the Other is a blank slate to be filled or an infant to be developed by the already developed world. Rather, it assumes that all worlds have treasures to share.

Story 3: Graduate School at Vanderbilt University

In 1992, when I started my graduate studies at Vanderbilt University, I was struck by the language requirements and the implications of these requirements. I was required to take *Koine* Greek and biblical Hebrew at an intermediate level regardless of my prior background. I was also required to take classical Greek and two European languages. So I began with classical Greek. I read and translated the likes of Plato and Aristotle, and found that to be a very nasty hiking trip to ancient Greece. I spent many hours agonizing with the dead white men of ancient Greece. I was not amused. Then I completed intermediate *Koine* Greek, which was not that gruesome since I had already done Greek to intermediate levels at the University of Botswana and the University of Durham. This was followed by elementary and intermediate Hebrew language study. In the four semesters of my course work and summers, I was overdosed with language courses. But it was not over. As a biblical scholar, I was also required to do two of the following European languages: French, Spanish, or German. I registered for French and took it during the summer.

I was now ready for my qualifying exams, or almost! I had one more European language to take. That's when I said to myself, "English is my first European language and I don't think I need to take another." I argued that for most white students from the United States, English was their mother tongue. But my mother tongue is Ndebele, and English was the first European language I learned. Fortunately, my advisor supported my argument and I was exempted from studying another European language.

The whole process of learning the required languages in biblical studies was an arduous journey of being colonized. I had registered for New Testament studies and here I was fully baptized into classical Greek, *Koine* Greek, and French, and threatened with German or Spanish. These languages were languages of the empires, ancient and modern. It was not enough that I grew up having to do all my education in the English language, the language of the colonizer, and I had to spend my life writing in English; to be a solid New Testament scholar, I also had to drink my fill in the history of domination. I had to learn and uphold the languages of the former colonizers whether I liked it or not. I felt that to become a New Testament scholar I had to be further alienated from African cultures, languages, and history, and to be baptized into ancient and modern imperial cultures and history. It was a bitter drink, the vinegar of colonial crucifixion.

The language requirements I had to fulfill at Vanderbilt University were typical of most, if not all, of the academic departments of biblical studies in the United States. While such language and history requirements may seem normal to the white students from the West, for those from the Two-Thirds World, they are undoubtedly Eurocentric. Thus, more often than not, New Testament studies means studying the Roman Empire and classical Greek and how the Jewish people were shaped by these empires. The language and historical background requirements do not consider that there are other cultures, languages, and histories of the Bible that may be important for students from different backgrounds. In the process, the programs have become so Eurocentric that students from the Two-Thirds World learn nothing about the histories that brought the Bible to their lands, the languages of translations, or the methods of reading the Bible in their contexts.

It is imperative that biblical studies programs in general should begin to shift from their Eurocentric focus to consider the languages, cultures, and histories of the Two-Thirds World. Such a curriculum transformation would require that biblical studies programs begin to determine what are the most critical languages, cultures, and histories for those from Africa, Latin America, and Asia. Such a quest would entail gathering biblical scholars from all regions to assess how biblical studies programs have been designed thus far and how they need to be transformed to move away from the colonizing ideological boundaries of the Eurocentric/Western framework.

For example, drawing on an African background, biblical studies could highlight ancient Egypt and how it shaped biblical traditions. Coptic languages, diasporic histories of Africa, and the role of the Bible in the colonial history of the church could be incorporated into the curriculum. Also critical to the enrichment of the curriculum would be the inclusion of the study of colonial history and its impact on Bible translations. The translation of the Bible into the four sub-Saharan languages in the context of colonial history and the subsequent postindependence Bible translations would offer insights into the history of the colonial missions that brought the Bible. The curriculum could also explore the continuity or discontinuity between colonial readings and contemporary biblical interpretations.

Such a mapping should be done for each continent and made available in all programs of biblical studies. So far, the program of biblical studies has been designed to fit a Eurocentric/Western straightjacket of one size fits all. It is clearly a colonial map, whose boundaries have been carefully drawn to keep the "Third World" out of biblical studies, for its unreserved inclusion might lower the standard of what constitutes "proper" biblical studies. For some of us from the Two-Thirds World, studying in the so-called developed world has been an experience of massive exclusion. We have been given bitter vinegar to drink when we sought a drink that would quench our thirst. The journey of "Discovering the Bible in the non-Biblical World," as Kwok Pui-lan put it, is a journey yet to be undertaken in biblical studies.

One thing that struck me, however, is that the Graduate School of Religion at Vanderbilt, on the cutting edge of scholarship, has shifted from historical methods of inquiry. For example, while we were subjected to rigorous language requirements, there were few times, if any at all, that we were expected to put these languages to use according to the dictates of traditional scholarship. The question arises as to what drives schools to continue to require languages that are no longer applicable, even at schools that have shifted their approach to biblical studies? This points to a larger issue. What are the accreditation standards for a solid program of biblical studies? The accrediting agencies and the standards they have established need to be revisited and decolonized because they continue to reinforce standards of theological studies that are circumscribed by colonizing boundaries.

Story 4: The Other at the Claremont Graduate University (CGU) School of Religion

This particular analysis was part of my "Postcolonial and Feminism" class that I taught at Scripps College and the Graduate School of Religion at Claremont in the fall semester of 2004. The students' assignment was to assess how their programs of study had been decolonized. Consequently, I carried out a brief examination of the School of Religion's representations of the Other as described in its program book, which highlights potential areas of curriculum transformation. The areas I examined are the educators, the content of the program, and its implications.

The faculty members at the Claremont Graduate School of Religion are, for the most part, products of universities such as Yale, Harvard, Columbia, McGill, Emory, Princeton, Duke, Vanderbilt, and Claremont. A majority have been trained within North America. Is this a subtle ideology of keeping out the dangerous "Third World"? In the case of ethnicity, and insofar as I could determine from names, there were some sprinkles of diversity. In general, the Other is seemingly kept to the minimum like those supposedly underdeveloped and dangerous drugs from the Third World. The make-up of the teaching staff is therefore a central part of monitoring and maintaining colonial boundaries.

The academic program was divided into six areas of concentration: (1) Hebrew Bible, (2) New Testament, (3) Philosophy of Religion and Theology, (4) History of Christianity and Religions in North America, (5) Women's Studies in Religion, and (6) Theology, Ethics, and Culture. Upon recent examination, I have found the addition of a master's program in Jewish and Islamic studies, which was not there at the time of my earlier analysis. There were areas of specialization within each of the stated concentrations with six sections listed for each course. Claremont has a solid program and the school ranks very high nationally.

Be that as it may, the academic programs are built around the biblical traditions, Christian theology, its Western privileged contexts, a somewhat Western focused history of Christianity, and various schools of philosophical thought. Confucianism, Buddhism, Hinduism, and Islam are mentioned in relation to women's studies in religion, but when I checked the number of courses offered I found them on the periphery. They are there, but they exist on the margins of the space. I could not find much, if any, on Native American religions, theology, or philosophy. I found one course on African religions, even less on African theologies, histories of African Christianity, or African philosophies. The same applied to Asia and Latin America together with their diasporas.

I am sure that some professors include sections from some of these areas in their syllabi. But by and large it seems that the Other in the story of CGU School of Religion remains just where the colonial cartographer drew the ideological boundaries: the Other is an infant with nothing of quality to offer and can actually endanger and compromise quality. Consequently, whenever the Other is given space, it is a small space somewhere in the background. Her existence must oscillate around the powers that be, and make little or no threatening impact on the core program made up of the colonizing Christian constructs. Like those Third World drugs, the Other must be and is kept out. If admitted at all, she or he must be admitted with caution, fully aware that this is not good for the American people.

Story 5: I Am at the University of Botswana; I Am in Africa

I want to share two stories from the University of Botswana (UB) and my experience during the time I worked for the World Council of Churches (WCC) as a gender and HIV&AIDS theological consultant.

In my final year as an undergraduate (1987/88) in Botswana, I took a course called TRS 402 — Twentieth-Century Theologians. It was a year-long course over two semesters. The first semester focused on European theologians such as Paul Tillich, Dietrich Bonhoeffer, Jürgen Moltman, Karl Barth, Rudolf Bultmann, and some Vatican II theologians. In the second semester the course covered what was called "Third World Theologians" and included African and Latin American theologians. I need not elaborate. This is an eloquent example of Eurocentrism in theological education and how the so-called Third World occupies a small, squeezed space where it more or less oscillates around the core of white Western theologies, methods, theories, and histories. In 2000/2001 UB carried out a massive curriculum review that entailed introducing semesters revisiting the contents of courses, phasing out some old ones, and designing new ones. Recently, when I checked out the new program I found that the course I took in 1987/88 has maintained its name, but its contents feature only white Western theologians, mostly German and the post–Vatican II Catholic theologians. The implication of the title and its contents is that there are no twentieth-century theologians from the Two-Thirds World. Between the first version of the course and the current one, I do not know which one is worse, but one thing is very clear: Eurocentrism reigns in both cases.

The context of my work with the World Council of Churches was in relation to HIV&AIDS education. This experience exposed the theological inadequacy of those who remained silent about the epidemic and those who responded verbally by arguing that HIV&AIDS is God's curse or punishment upon people living with HIV&AIDS. Since leaders in faith-based institutions were the proponents of the latter perspective, it was asked, "Who trains our faith leaders and who should retrain them?" While theological educators were identified as the trainers, most theological programs did not feature HIV&AIDS education in their curricula. Training had to begin at that level. Thus I ended up with the job as a gender and HIV&AIDS theological consultant.[16] My task was to gather academic theologians and scholars of religion from across Africa to facilitate a discussion to ascertain what they were doing about HIV&AIDS education in their programs and what they could do to mainstream HIV&AIDS education. The program assembled and trained 740 theological educators from all regions, save North Africa. The training involved re-assessing the response of theological institutions at policy, program, and course levels. The trainees spent five days working on areas where HIV&AIDS education could be mainstreamed into existing policy and courses, or in designing new courses and programs. The intention was to give academic theologians, scholars of religion, and other leaders ways and skills to mainstream HIV&AIDS education. At the end of the workshop, we evaluated our gathering by discussing the way forward, the possible challenges and hindrances we faced, and ways to address them.

During this process, I came to realize that many African theological programs are quite Eurocentric, for some of the following reasons:

- Many departments and programs were founded by Westerners who transported their programs to Africa.

- Most African theologians and scholars of religion are trained in the West (like me) and they are much more likely to maintain and reproduce the Eurocentric theological programs they themselves learned.

- Many of the theological programs are accredited by Western theological schools that then dictate the contents of the program as a condition for accreditation.

- Many theological programs are sponsored by institutions based in the West that use their economic power to dictate what passes as adequate theological education.

- Many faith-based theological institutions are overseen by a board comprising faith leaders who approve any changes, thus limiting and controlling the freedom of the professors in the area of curricular transformation.

Many of the trainees who attended the workshop said that they found the workshop very useful, but that they did not have the freedom to mainstream HIV&AIDS education in the existing courses or to design new ones. Of course, some were able to do so, and an evaluation of what transpired in the theological institutions of those who participated in this training program would be fruitful.

Conclusions

These stories underline the need for curricular transformation to de-colonize theological studies. The stories call for self-examination and for redrawing the boundaries of academic discourse. President Bush could say that he wanted to protect U.S. citizens from the dangerous "Third World" drugs because many departments, including theological programs, do indeed hold this view. I submit that the strongest and the most persistent marginalization of the Other exists within and is maintained by institutional structures, policies, and programs. These have become the gatekeepers of the colonial ideology with its patriarchy, racism, classism, homophobia, and many other forms of marginalizing the Other. The colonial ideology of subordination is embedded in many academic disciplines and departments as is attested by the inclusion of "Third World" only in a tourist sense.

Curricular transformation of theological education, no doubt, demands more than just politically correct language and equal opportunity policies from institutions. It demands more than just solidarity with those who are calling for change. It calls for accountability in establishing the necessary changes. While individual professors and students pushing for certain agendas in theological studies is vital, curricular transformation demands more than just a few courses on feminist, African American, Native American, Asian American, and Third World theologies and biblical hermeneutics.

Decolonizing theological studies calls for complete curricular transformation, which begins by assessing the whole program and its relationship to othering the Others. I think we all need to begin by reading our own stories and interrogating our training, our course content, and the composition of our faculties and academic programs in order to expose the underlying Eurocentric ideology of border-keeping. If we do, we will find the Other still largely othered. Many programs and subjects maintain their colonial and colonizing academic framework with Eurocentrism as its center, while the rest must oscillate around the periphery or be simply ignored. My hope is that theological practitioners and leaders will want to decolonize their frameworks and their programs by seeking to take up the challenge of R. S. Sugirtharajah: "There is no admission of the place of colonialism in the shaping of English theology" and "Western theologians have yet to offer a sustained theological analysis of the impact of colonialism."[17]

Notes

1. *The Postcolonial Biblical Reader* (Oxford: Blackwell, 2006), 18.

2. The term "Third World" has occupied different theoretical values among Two-Thirds World scholars, both positively and negatively. See R. S. Sugirtharajah, *The Bible and the Third World: Precolonial, Colonial and Postcolonial Encounters* (Cambridge: Cambridge University Press, 2001), 1–4.

3. Edward Said, *Orientalism* (London: Penguin, 1985); Ngugï Wa Thiong'o, *Decolonising the Mind: The Politics of Language in African Literature* (London:

J. Currey; Portsmouth, NH: Heinemann, 1986); V. Y. Mudimbe, *The Invention of Africa: Gnosis, Philosophy and the Order of Knowledge* (Bloomington: Indiana University Press, 1988); Ella Shohat and Robert Stam, *Unthinking Eurocentrism: Multiculturalism and the Media* (New York: Routledge, 1997).

4. Sugirtharajah, *The Postcolonial Biblical Reader,* 18–19.

5. Fernando Segovia, "And They Began to Speak in Other Tongues: Competing Modes of Discourse in Contemporary Biblical Criticism," in *Reading from This Place 1: Social Location and Biblical Interpretation in Global Perspective,* ed. Fernando Segovia and Mary Ann Tolbert (Minneapolis: Fortress Press, 1995), 1–32.

6. Musa Dube, "Postcolonial Biblical Interpretations," in *Methods of Biblical Interpretations,* ed. John H. Hayes (Nashville: Abingdon, 2004), 361–66.

7. Segovia, "And They Began to Speak in Other Tongues," 1–32.

8. Shohat and Stam, *Unthinking Eurocentrism,* 208.

9. Musa Dube, *Postcolonial Feminist Interpretations of the Bible* (St. Louis: Chalice Press, 2000), 169–84.

10. Musa Dube, "Reading for Decolonization (John 4:1–42)," *Semeia* 75 (1996): 37–59.

11. Dube, *Postcolonial Feminist Interpretations of the Bible,* 144–55.

12. Dube, "Reading for Decolonization (John 4:1–42)," 37–59.

13. Craig R. Koester, "The Savior of the World (John 4:42)," *Journal of Biblical Literature* 109 (1990): 665–80.

14. Dube, *Postcolonial Feminist Interpretations of the Bible,* 137.

15. Kwok Pui-lan, *Discovering the Bible in the Non-Biblical World* (Maryknoll, NY: Orbis Books, 1995), 19.

16. Musa Dube, ed., *HIV/AIDS and the Curriculum: Methods of Integrating HIV/AIDS in Theological Program* (Geneva: WCC, 2003); Musa Dube and Musimbi Kanyoro, eds., *Grant Me Justice: HIV/AIDS and Gender Readings of the Bible* (Pietermaritzburg: Cluster, 2004; Maryknoll, NY: Orbis Books, 2004); Musa Dube, *The HIV&AIDS Bible: Some Selected Essays* (Scranton, PA: University of Scranton Press, 2007).

17. Sugirtharajah, *The Postcolonial Biblical Reader,* 18–19.

8

"AWAKENING" TO A NEW APPROACH TO THE BIBLE

S. Wesley Ariarajah

I brought with me two different kinds of expertise when I joined Drew University Graduate and Theological Schools as the professor of ecumenical theology. Following my initial theological training, most of my postgraduate work was in the area of Hinduism and Hindu-Christian relations. I also had sufficient knowledge of other major religious traditions to be able to teach an introductory course on world religions. My other field was ecumenism. I have had more than thirty years of direct involvement with the work of the World Council of Churches, with sixteen of those years as staff person located in the WCC's headquarters in Geneva. The experience and knowledge acquired during that period helped me to offer issue-centered courses in ecumenism.

I begin with this personal note because it has much to do with the rest of this essay. This is not a scholarly article on biblical hermeneutics, but rather a story of "hermeneutical experience," if our academic rhetoric can accommodate such a formulation! Unfortunately, the story falls short of what it needs to be elevated to such status as "comparative theology," "inter-textual hermeneutics" or "inter-cultural hermeneutics." What I hope to do is to discuss two of my courses, one on ecumenical theology and the other on world religions and how these two courses, in an unlikely combination, had an impact on my students, especially on their attitudes and approach to the Bible.

But first some background information on the students. The student body at Drew Theological School is drawn from many denominations and from all parts of the United States and abroad. They represent a great variety of theological traditions within the Christian church. Perhaps the only thing they have in common, next to the variety of ways of expressing some commitment to Jesus Christ, is the Bible. Even those who are not too familiar with the contents of the Bible believe that (in one sense or another) it is the "Word of God." The conservative among them come with more definitive beliefs, such as the "inerrancy of Scriptures" and the "infallibility" of the Bible, based on the conviction that the scriptures are "divinely inspired." I am aware that these views are tested by fire in their required courses on the Hebrew and Christian scriptures, where all the old and new critical tools are employed to understand the text and its meaning.

It is no secret that there are three kinds of responses to a critical study of the Bible in these classes. Many who come as "Bible-believing Christians" gradually develop an informed understanding of the nature of scriptures and begin to own, use, and celebrate the Bible in new ways. Another part of the student body begins to live in two worlds — the world of the classroom, where they go along with all the new "stuff" in order to get a good grade for the courses and a protected world of "personal faith" where the Bible is given the status and authority, and a particular approach to reading it, that had first convinced them of the truth of the Christian faith. Despite all that is learned in the classroom, it is too threatening for them to "let go" of the attitude to the Bible with which they first entered the seminary. The third group, a minority, whose faith is so dependent on the Bible being the divinely inspired inerrant Word of God, experiences a spiritual crisis that continues almost to the end of their training period.

These trends became more apparent to me in my course, "Scripture and Tradition: Ecumenical Advances." Here we first study the origins and nature of the biblical material, the development of the biblical canon, and the different approaches to the Bible and its authority within the churches that are part of the ecumenical movement. Second, we study (using the documents of the WCC's Faith and Order Commission) the discussions on the relationship between scripture and tradition, the divisions among the churches on this question, and some of the ecumenical advances that have been made through common study and reflection. This course also attempts to help the students develop fresh approaches to both scripture and tradition. But on the whole, one would still discern the three types of responses mentioned above in relation to biblical studies. The difficulty has to do with five assumptions about the Bible that are central to many Protestant Christians:

1. The Bible is the commonly held and widely accepted authority of the Christian faith; it sets the boundaries of our faith; once we begin to cast doubts about its status and authority, we begin the process of undermining the faith.

2. For the Bible to have such authority, one has to accept it, in one sense or another, as "divinely inspired." If we do not give it some such status, why would people want to use it as their "Holy Scripture"; why would these books, written centuries ago, have any spiritual authority to the people of our day?

3. This also means that we should give some intrinsic authority to the Bible itself and what it teaches directly on specific issues. It is natural that people have meditated, reflected upon, and interpreted the Bible over the centuries, but these can only be inspirational in our own spiritual quest. The commentaries and interpretations given by people must be seen for what they are. The Bible speaks for itself.

4. The Bible attests to the truth of the Christian faith, the nature of the salvation God has offered to humankind, God's self-revelation in Jesus Christ, and the ultimate destiny of human life. There is no other source to which we can turn in order to give credibility to what we believe. Therefore there should be some limits to the questioning of its nature and authority.

5. As people come up with new teachings, doctrines, ethical values, and orientations on personal, social, and political life, the only common touchstone we have to test them is the Bible. If we completely tear it apart and treat it as a culturally and historically bound document that has no authority of faith in our day, we will eventually totally undermine our faith.

These five reservations are my own summary of the many comments made in discussions on the Bible and its authority in the classroom on ecumenical theology. There were arguments for and against all the above, but I will not attempt to elaborate on them in this short essay.

It is in this context that I wish to turn to the course I teach on world religions. The title I have given to this required course is "Challenge of World Religions to Christian Faith and Practice." The intention of the title is to indicate that we will attempt not only to study some of the beliefs and practices of other religious traditions, but also to ask ourselves the question, "What light do they throw on our own faith and practices?" In other words, the course has a dialogical element built into it so that Christians can learn about other faiths and practices by asking the question, "How can this particular understanding enrich, enliven, correct, or question what we believe?" The course is designed and taught in such a way that the students are led to formulate answers to this question for themselves without having to verbalize them in public. But from time to time, however, they do engage in open conversations in the classroom.

What I hope to do in this essay is to show how the study of scriptures, their authority, and their use in *other* religious traditions have brought greater transformation in students' attitudes and approach to the Bible than anything else that is learned in my class on "Scripture and Tradition."

Religions without Scriptures

The first existential shock for the students early in the course is the realization that there are religious traditions that have no scriptures at all, and that scripture is not the hallmark of being a religious tradition. Even though most students have a vague knowledge of this reality, they confront it squarely when they begin to look at some other traditions. For example, the Native American and many of the African religious traditions have no written scriptures at all. Yet they are able to cohere as traditions, organize their spiritual life and practices, and hold up ethical and moral values without having to resort to scriptural authority. We still have to look for ways in which these elements are negotiated and handed down within these religious communities, but the very realization that they have no "scriptures" is powerful in demystifying the place of scriptures.

Students also begin to see that scriptures become important in religions that have founders, and especially when such founding is linked to special revelations. A canon of scripture becomes important to preserve the story of the founders and their basic teachings; this is particularly true when they are threatened with distortion and dilution. This is a special burden to "world" religions that spreads beyond the cultural, geographical, and sociopolitical contexts of their origins. Many of them have to attribute Divine Authority/Revelation to their scriptures so that they are accepted without questioning in the many cultures and contexts into which the religion moves.

Which Scriptures?

All the rules about Christian understandings of scriptures break down when we come to the Hindu tradition. There is a plentitude of texts that come under the general notion of "Hindu Scriptures." Although the Vedas, Upanishads, and the Bhagavadgita enjoy special authority in general, a vast corpus of mythology (*puranas*), *agamic* and *tantric* literature, and great epics (*itihasas*) like *Mahabharatha* and *Ramayana* are also considered scriptures. In addition, a considerable corpus of materials in the vernacular languages is also considered authoritative by specific sections of the Hindu society. The devotional songs of Alvars (devotees of Vishnu) and Nayanmars (devotees of Shiva) are perhaps the only scriptures that are familiar to those who make Vishnu or Shiva the focus of their devotion.

The Vedas and the Upanishads (which strictly are also part of the Vedas) are considered "revealed" scriptures. However, the word "reveal" does not imply what is meant in the Christian and Islamic traditions. The Vedas are designated *Śruti*, which literally means "that which is heard," or in a broader sense, that which is experienced, while all other scriptures are considered *Smriti*, meaning "that which is remembered." *Śruti* is primary because it is a form of direct experience, whereas *Smriti* is secondary since it is a recollection of that experience.

Students find it difficult to figure out why the "revealed" scriptures are not simply called "revealed." This is also true of the Qur'an, which is considered a revelation, but was all "heard" by the Prophet. It is also difficult for them to understand why what was "heard" cannot be considered "revealed." I give an example to explain what is intended: Supposing I "see" a car accident as I walk along the road; I have one kind of knowledge of it, a more direct form. When I return home and tell my wife about the accident, she also gains knowledge of it but only through my remembrance. There is a qualitative difference between the two types of knowledge. That which came from my "experiencing" is more direct, more authoritative. What my wife "heard" also participates in the same knowledge of the same subject, but is not so direct and therefore cannot be as authoritative as the knowledge that came from the act of "experiencing." Therefore, the word "revealed" in Hinduism does not mean some kind of knowledge that was communicated from heaven, but a knowledge that arises from the immediacy of spiritual experience that the ancient *rishis* appear to have had in their attempts to be in communion with the Divine. But does this mean that the Vishnava and Saiva saints, who sang songs of such great devotion, did not have the same immediacy of communion with the Divine? When this question is put to Hindus, they will respond that the authority of the Vedas arises not only from their status as "heard" but also because they are the oldest scriptures and have been remembered and passed down for more than three thousand years.

It is also of interest that the Bhagavadgita, which is of much later origin, is elevated almost to the level of the Vedas, and is considered, along with the Upanishads, as part of the informal "triple canon" of Hindu orthodoxy. This means that the requirement for scriptures to be considered "authoritative" depends more on their inner authority to elicit acceptance than on some external proof that they were "given" or have "descended" from heaven. It is also of interest that most of the Hindus do not know the text of the Vedas, nor are they expected to know them in order to be considered Hindus. They do not look to the Vedas and the Upanishads for ethical and moral guidance in living their lives. Much of the Vedic texts are memorized in their original language of Sanskrit by priests who use them in rituals. The Upanishadic parts of the Vedas provide the basis or the starting point for much of the Hindu philosophic reflections, and the Bhagavadgita, along with the epics, provides the inspiration for Hindu conduct.

Thus, even though the Vedas, Upanishads, and the Bhagavadgita carry greater authority in comparison to other scriptures, they do not nullify the others. In fact, a vast number of Hindus look to other parts of the scriptural tradition as authoritative. Much later teachings, like those of Ramakrishna Paramahamsa, Vallalar, and others, are raised by sections of the Hindu community to scriptural status because of the spiritual authority they carry in themselves. And most Hindus who live deeply devoted lives may never have read a single page of any of what are considered scriptures within their tradition. This expansive attitude, and even a lack of any attitude, toward scriptures has in no way undermined Hinduism as a religion, or the authentic spirituality of many who live by that tradition. This phenomenon challenges those who hold that the truth of their religion would stand or fall depending on the authority given (or not given) to their scriptures.

By studying about Hindu scriptures the students begin to see the complexity of what is involved in considering something as having scriptural authority. Do the teachings in the book of Leviticus and in the Sermon on the Mount have the same authority to a Christian because the whole Bible is believed to be "revealed"? Or do we, unofficially, live with our own canons within the canon? In what sense is the Bible authoritative? Is it because it was given by the Divine? Is it because it comes out of an immediacy of experience on the part of those who wrote it? Is it because it has an intrinsic power to elicit authority?

How Many Canons
Can a Religion's Scriptures Have?

When we turn to Buddhism we are introduced to a whole new concept of scriptures and canon. Since Buddhism, like Christianity and Islam, is also a founded religion, sometime after the demise of the Buddha there arose the need to preserve an authentic account of his life and teachings. Ulrich Pagel gives an account of what the tradition says about it:

> For this purpose, Mahakasyapa, a prominent disciple of the Buddha, reportedly convened a council in Rajagraha, the capital of Magadha. He appointed five hundred *arahants* (accomplished monks free of all attachments) to check the authenticity of the teachings submitted to the council. For the doctrine he called on Ananda, the Buddha's personal attendant known to have heard most sermons, to recite all the discourses (*sutta*) he remembered. For the monastic code, Mahakasyapa summoned Upali, great expert in the *Vinaya,* and asked him to relate all monastic rules he heard from the Buddha's lips. Before a discourse or a precept was formally authenticated, it was subjected to careful scrutiny and

required unanimous approval by all five hundred *arahants*. Whenever in doubt, the assembly refused admission out of fear that they
unwittingly might alter the Buddha's teaching.[1]

The historical veracity of the accounts of the conference is open to
question, but there is no doubt that sometime soon after the Buddha's
death his disciples attempted to collect and preserve the tradition. If such
careful work was indeed done, of all the religious traditions of the world,
Buddhism should have a clearly defined, authoritative, and commonly
accepted canon of scripture to which all Buddhists subscribe.

What the students soon find out when studying and seeking to understand its scriptures is that Buddhism is perhaps the most complex
religion. When Buddhism began to expand eastward into Sri Lanka,
Myanmar, Thailand, and Indochina, and northward into Tibet, China,
and on from there to Korea, Japan, and the neighboring nations, in the
true spirit of Buddhism, it "let go" of both the Buddha and the scriptures! The buddhas of the Mahayana tradition of Tibet and of the Pure
Land tradition of Japan have little resemblance to the original Buddha
of North India. Further, as Buddhism moved into other lands, "new"
scriptures arose on the basis of the original texts. These scriptures ran
into hundreds of volumes and were written down (in addition to the
original Pali) in Sanskrit, Tibetan, Chinese, Korean, Japanese, and so
on, making it impossible for anyone to really know much of the "Buddhist scriptures" without studying a number of languages. The capacity
of a tradition to "let go" of its scriptures as part of its mission, and
the readiness to accept as "scriptures" the many expansions of the basic
teachings (sometimes with considerable liberty) is quite a new experience
to the students. They are aware that the Bible is the book that has been
translated into the greatest number of languages of the world. However,
it is always the official canon that has been translated, mostly from the
original Hebrew and Greek so that no word is added or taken out of
the canon.

What is of interest in Buddhism is that there are also multiple canons:
a Pali canon, a Sanskrit canon, a Chinese canon, and so on, in the re-
spective languages, carrying many more writings than were acceptable
to Mahakasyapa's first gathering in Magadha. Yet they are deemed to
be about the same person and his teachings. Buddhism demystifies the

concept of canon, and transforms it from a rigid and unalterable textual prison into an agreed-upon collection of texts that can serve as the spiritual storehouse to the faith community in a given place.

The Unalterable Words of God

Students move into a more familiar, yet a deeply challenging situation when they study Islam. "The Qur'an, in Islamic thinking, is not only the Word of God, but also the words of God" I tell the students, "and it had to be given by the angel Gabriel directly to the Prophet because the previous revelations of God through Moses and Jesus had been corrupted by Jews and Christians." In Islamic thinking, the Qur'an is not "inspired," but was given directly, word by word, to the Prophet, and his responsibility was only to "recite" the words to the people. Some Muslims argue that Prophet Muhammad had to be an unlettered person so that the message of God would not be distorted by his own thinking. Further, in the strict sense, the Qur'an cannot be translated because the poetic beauty and the rhythm of the Arabic language in which it was revealed are also part of its essence. Therefore, all over the world Muslims commit to memory and recite the Qur'an in the original Arabic, even if they do not always understand the meaning of the Arabic words.

The place and significance of the Qur'an can be fully appreciated only when we understand Islamic anthropology. There is no concept of original sin in Islam. Every child born into the world is a Muslim, not in a sectarian sense but in the sense that his or her heart is turned in submission to God, and the child, from the time of its birth, is destined to be in Paradise. But in the course of its life it can go astray and live a life that diverts it from Paradise and takes it to the paths of hell. Therefore, God, out of God's mercy and compassion, has revealed God's will for humankind so that they might walk in the right path. Hence the need for the direct revelation of God's will for personal, social, economic, and political life. Like the Jewish people's attitude to the Torah, Muslims do not see the Qur'an as a form of book of law but rather as a gift from God to direct our lives in the paths of righteousness.

Students begin to see the vast contrast in approaches to scriptures in Buddhism and Islam, and some of them begin to feel that Islam might be taking the concept of revelation a bit too far for their liking, only to be reminded that perhaps there are parallel tendencies in their own approaches to the Bible. For the first time, they are also confronted not simply with internal dissent over the Bible among Christians, but with a whole tradition that holds Jesus in great respect, but sees the Christian scriptures to have been corrupted to such an extent that God had to reveal God's will all over again. How does one handle competing claims to final revelation?

The Inexhaustible Search

When we begin the study of Judaism, many Christians demonstrate a surprising level of ignorance of the very tradition from which they have emerged. Most Christians think that if they know the "Old Testament" they know Judaism. The first task of the teacher is to introduce Rabbinic Judaism, and to insist that we should look upon Judaism as a contemporary religious tradition like any other. Most students do not have any idea of how the Jewish people regard and use the Torah. Part of the confusion arises from the Jewish tradition's own use of the word "Torah." In a strict sense, since the Torah is believed to have been given by God to Moses, it should denote, as it in fact does, the five Books of Moses (Pentateuch). But then the rest of the Hebrew Bible, which includes the *nebî'îm* (prophets) and the *ketubîm* (writings), is also referred to as the Torah. Further, the Jewish tradition deeply respects the interpretative traditions of the Torah known as the Talmud and refers to them as the "Oral Torah." The Oral Torah is held in as much respect as the written Torah. Christian students who come from churches deeply divided over the interpretation of the Bible have much difficulty in accepting that the interpretative traditions can have as much authority as the written Torah. Whose interpretation do we accept? How do we agree that one interpretation is more authentic than another? But the Jewish tradition is firm on affirming the Oral Torah and its importance is illustrated by a rabbinic story told of the first-century sage Hillel:

> Once a would-be-convert came to Hillel and asked to be converted to Judaism, but the heathen [*sic*] wanted to accept only the Written Scripture not the Oral Teachings. Hillel, surprisingly, agreed to accept him as a convert and began to teach him the Hebrew alphabet so that he could study the written text. Next day Hillel continued with the lesson but this time he taught him the alphabet

in the reverse order. The heathen objected, and Hillel replied that he wanted to show him that even to read the written text he needed to rely on oral teachings. How much more would this be true if he wanted to *understand* the written teaching? (TB *Shabbat* 31a)[2]

We view a video of Jewish rabbinic candidates studying the Torah in an Orthodox Jewish seminary. It functions like a noisy market place as seen in some parts of the world where everyone is arguing with one another to beat down prices. The Torah is studied in twos, with the text and the Talmud, which carries the opinions and the arguments on the text over the centuries. Serious arguments, including raising of the voices to higher pitches, takes place, all to get at the meaning of what the text is saying to someone at a particular moment. The written Torah (Hebrew Bible) is given; we cannot change it. In fact, the scrolls of the Torah, before they are read, are taken in procession in the synagogue with great devotion, people reaching out to touch and kiss them. In Jewish thinking, the Torah is the greatest gift God has given to humankind. But there can be no single interpretation of its meaning; many interpretations are better. God has given us intelligence to argue out its meaning and its significance for us today, and everything that our forbearers and the great scholars have said will help in our search for meaning. In other words, there is no end to the meanings that we can draw out of the text of the Bible, and it is important that we disagree, argue over, and struggle with the text, seeking all the help we can get, to find its meaning. In fact, it is believed that if the Torah were self-evident and needed no interpretation, there would be no need for preaching or seminary education.

Most students who are exposed for the very first time to the understanding and approach to scriptures within Judaism are overwhelmed by the liberty Jewish people take in the area of interpretation. The impact is significant because it relates to much of what they consider to be their scripture as well.

"Awakening" to a New Understanding of the Bible and Its Authority

The impact the course has on the student needs no elaboration here. In the courses in biblical studies and my "Scripture and Tradition" class in ecumenical theology, students are opened up to new ways of looking at the Bible. But many initially experience it as an attack on the Bible. Their first response is to resist in silence, and often a change in perspective comes only through a painful process of unlearning and sorting out the positions with which they began. Some students, to the very end, have a sense of having lost something by moving away from their initial approach to the scriptures. And a few even lose their link to the scriptures because of not knowing other ways to relate to the Bible.

It is at this point that the course on world religions comes to their help. In it students have a kind of "awakening," not dissimilar to what happened to the Lord Buddha under the Bodhi tree. Suddenly they become aware that we are not the only ones that base our faith on scriptures. Then they see a whole new array of ways in which scripture and its authority are understood within other traditions, and they understand that it is possible to have a deep and profound spiritual life without having to be imprisoned by one particular way of looking at scriptures. They discover profoundly different ways in which scriptures can help a faith community to deepen its spiritual life. Students are never asked to verbalize the transformation that takes place, but I have no doubt that they no longer relate to the Bible in the way they previously did.

Notes

1. Ulrich Pagel, "Buddhism," in *Sacred Writings,* ed. Jean Holm and John Bowker (London: Pinter Publisher, 1994), 12–13.

2. Alan Unterman, "Judaism" in *Sacred Writings,* ed. Jean Holm and John Bowker (London: Pinter Publisher, 1994), 129.

PART FOUR

PERSONAL PERSPECTIVES

9

MARGINS AND MAINSTREAM

An Interview with R. S. Sugirtharajah

D. N. Premnath

In the initial stages of conceptualizing this volume in honor of the work of R. S. Sugirtharajah, my first thought was to have it be a surprise. But after conversations with colleagues, I realized that a volume devoted to cross-cultural hermeneutics would be lacking without some contribution from the scholar who has written extensively on this matter and whose works have inspired many other scholars around the world. As a result, I have asked Sugi to comment directly on various innovations in biblical studies since he began work in this area.

I have known Sugi since 1975, when we were contemporaries at the United Theological College in Bangalore, India. I was getting my bachelor of divinity degree, and Sugi, his master of theology. I still remember vividly the serious conversations about christological issues, Indian Christian theological voices, and, in a lighter vein, skits that Sugi used to write, parodying or poking fun at the faculty at the college. In the following decades, although we went our separate paths, we followed each other's work and well-being. I watched in admiration his continued foray into new forms of knowledge as he sought to enrich biblical and theological hermeneutics. As I look back on our association over the years, it is heartening to see that Sugi has found his niche in the arena of biblical hermeneutics. His works interfacing postcolonialism and biblical studies have opened up an exciting avenue of biblical interpretation and appropriation. I greatly appreciate this opportunity to learn his reactions to this approach to biblical hermeneutics.

153

You were responsible for bringing out two landmark volumes —
Voices from the Margin *and* The Postcolonial Biblical Reader.
*There is a fifteen-year gap between the two. What sort of changes
do you see between these two publications?*

The first obvious change is in the context. These two volumes were trying to meet the hermeneutical needs of two very different situations.
Voices, in that first edition, came at a time when liberation theology
was at its peak. Spurred on and influenced by Latin American liberation
theology, a number of theologies developed — such as Korean *minjung*
theology, the Filipino theology of struggle, and Third World feminist
theologies — that incorporated liberation motifs into their articulations.
Most of the articles in that volume reflected the optimism and hope of
this liberative thrust. *The Postcolonial Biblical Reader* reflects a change
of mood in the production of theological knowledge. Postcolonialism
shifted the theological emphasis from solely economic forms of domination to cultural and intellectual forms. It grappled not only with the
issues surrounding the consequences of colonialism, but also with the
challenges of multiculturalism and the problems faced by ethnic minorities. With this new departure, cultural and intellectual liberation provide
a more comprehensive basis for doing theology.

A second change is in the status and standing of the Bible. *Voices*
ended up making the Bible a neat, uncomplicated, and unambiguous
book in spite of some unsavory aspects. The essays in *Voices* reinforced
and reinvigorated the authority of the Bible. In its own idiosyncratic
way, *Voices* encouraged a single, definitive, and at times triumphalistic
reading of the text, whereas the *Reader* makes the Bible a more complex
and ambiguous book. It is more interested in opening up the text than
in establishing its religious purity and authenticity. It is concerned with
textual ambivalences and encourages plural readings where no single
reading can be regarded as exhaustive.

Third, there are differences in design and reception. *Voices* was (and
still is) a much-used classroom text that significantly resonated with the
aspirations and tastes of university, seminary, and college students and
teachers of that time, who included a large proportion of ethnic minorities and women. It was the time of globalization of theological education
in North America, and *Voices* provided examples of how the other half
exegeted and interpreted. On the other hand, the *Reader's* main target is

Western scholarship, and it offers significant correctives to some of the imbalances and injustices in the construction of knowledge. The *Reader's* principal targets are the producers of knowledge in the West, and it challenges them to re-perceive how knowledge about the "other" is studied and codified. It thus provides a critical assessment of the intellectual articulation of the West's engagement with the "other."

Finally, there is a difference in the profile of the contributors. Almost all the contributions for *Voices* came from former colonies. In the case of the *Reader,* the essayists were from both the old and new imperial centers as well as from ex-colonies — a fulfillment of the hope anticipated in the Fanonian third phase.

You were one of those in the field of biblical studies to introduce the concept of the margins, and to situate your work on the margins. What do you think is happening to the margins now?

The margin I espoused then has taken a different turn today. I saw the margin as a place of discussion, dissent, and resistance. It has now become not only a menacing place but one crammed with protesters of spurious intent. It has become a haven for all those religious fundamentalists who claim that they have been pushed to the margins. The interpretation taking place there now is not a critical engagement with the text but a filching of selected texts to support a narrow religious vision.

The resistance offered from the margin has also perceptively changed. It is these religious fundamentalists who are now at the forefront of resistance. Previously, Enlightenment values were employed against tyranny and superstition, but now the benefits of modernity are used to reinforce totalitarianism and superstition. This is a good example of how those at the margin can aggressively use mainstream arguments to establish and bolster their case. More worryingly, the resistance that is offered is not secular and humanistic but is based on a warped teleology. Marginality is not to be "gloried in," as is now the case, but has to be brought to an end, so that the victims of economic, racial, sexual, and gender oppression can be set free.

How did you first get interested in postcolonial studies? What was the most influential factor that moved you in that direction?

I was looking for a critical framework worked out by "Third World" scholars that could hold its own amid other critical categories dominant in the academic discourse at that time. Most of the critical categories of that period, such as postmodernism and poststructuralism, were concerned with and emerged as a way of answering the questions encountered by the West. I was searching for a theory that could respond academically to some of the cultural, textual, and hermeneutical problems faced by Third World interpreters. As with many others, it was Edward Said's book *Orientalism* that initiated me into this area. The book introduced to a wide audience how scholarship operates. One of the most powerful ideas to filter through — a thought that has become so commonplace now — was the idea that what passes for scholarship has actually to do with who has the power to articulate it.

The book also pointed out the complicated relationship between the claim to disinterested scholarship and its complicit link with Western imperialism, and the way each fortified the other. It also made us aware of the nature of representation — how the "other" is individually and/or collectively portrayed. It opened up a new way of looking at our cultures and their relationship to the West. The book, as you know, is not immaculate and it has its faults. Said himself acknowledged this and tried to rectify them in the book's subsequent editions.

One of the important revisions introduced in his later writings has to do with resistance as a form of critical activity. The agency of the colonized and the resistance discourse that emerged as a response to colonialism are seen as constitutive of the colonial encounter. The colonized were not mute consumers; they also spoke and wrote back. *Orientalism* initiated what is known as colonial discourse analysis. This resulted in a number of scholars looking at colonial intentions and traces in literary texts, historical documents, and so forth. These ideas and insights of Said led me to situate biblical texts in their imperial contexts and to see how imperialism influenced biblical interpretation. The phrase of Kenyan writer Ngugi, "decolonizing the mind," in a way sums up the postcolonial agenda. Recently, when examining a doctoral dissertation, I discovered that the Indian theologian Stanley Samartha used an almost identical phrase back in the 1970s.

What particular aspects of postcolonial criticism have enriched biblical studies? And how?

Postcolonial criticism has enriched biblical studies in a number of ways. First, it has reanimated an interest in empire and put empire at the center of many biblical narratives. Various empires from the Assyrian to the Roman provided the context for several biblical books and supplied the social, cultural, and political framework. Mainstream scholarship limited our choice of study on this topic to its theological, spiritual, and historical aspects, but postcolonialism offered a counter-story by introducing the empire's presence in the texts and the implications that this carried.

Second, postcolonialism has exposed the stereotypical images in Western biblical scholarship of the cultures and peoples of the Orient. Even liberal scholarship has not escaped such misinterpretation, as I have shown in some of my writings.

Third, hermeneutical excavation undertaken by postcolonial criticism has uncovered the creative way the colonized have used the Bible. Situating themselves within the biblical history of salvation, the colonized were able to justify both their resistance to colonial rule and their defense of their disparaged culture. These resistance discourses have unearthed alternative voices that have invariably been hidden, suppressed, discredited, or discounted.

Fourth, the concerns that have come in the aftermath of colonialism, such as migrancy, diaspora, and hybridity, have been taken up by postcolonialism and used as a way of mining the texts for new meanings.

Fifth, at a time of specialization, postcolonialism has introduced generalists who can traverse different disciplines and see connections. More significantly, its interrogative readings have dented the righteous authority accorded to Western interpretations and demanded more academic accountability.

There is a tendency among members of the biblical guild to dismiss some of the newer methods by racial/ethnic scholars as exotic, not rigorous, and not of much scholarly value to mainstream biblical studies. How do you respond to this?

It all depends on what you mean by scholarly. In the context of the biblical guild, "scholarly" usually means sustaining or preserving certain concerns and interests, replicating particular sets of values, and reinforcing certain power relations. The mention of scholarly is a camouflage for power exercised by a few. It also means promoting an insider writing style that involves complicated phrases and syntax with a view to excluding the outsider. The writings of racial or ethnic scholars come out of their life-experiences of being vilified and demeaned. Their writings therefore reveal a great deal of emotion, passion, and expressions of anger, and they may at times seem confrontational. Such personal reflective discourse is not seen as a "proper" way of articulating theology. These scholars unashamedly and openly declare their presuppositions and preferential options, and this irritates and annoys those who believe that one should avoid these subjective articulations and engage in a "rational" discussion. Some of our works are dubbed lamentations.

"Scholarly" is also code for taking seriously only the Enlightenment and modernity, namely, the historical-critical method. But outside the historical method is an entire world that has given new impetus to interpretation. Some of the most exciting work of racial and ethnic scholars draws upon the orality, myths, and folklore originating from their communities, which has a disturbing effect on the mainstream.

In your work, you talk about "diasporic interpreters." What can you say about this group? What is their specific contribution?

This is a new phenomenon that has arisen over the last two decades. We see a sizeable group of Asians, Latinos, and Afro-Caribbeans, both first and second generation, making their presence felt in the academy and the publishing world. Their writings have demonstrated that one's place of origin is no longer a necessary reference point for doing hermeneutics. One can reflect theologically about India or Hong Kong away from these places. These diasporic interpreters represent a new breed of professionally trained scholars addressing and challenging the academy. Their works show how they constantly translate in both directions — from the home they left behind and the new home they are trying to make sense of.

In the early stages, it was an attempt to preserve what they had left behind and to keep those ideas alive in order to make sense of their transplanted lives in an environment that was at times hostile or apathetic. More than a linguistic exercise, it was a hermeneutical act for them. These interpreters were able to put new questions to the texts, and their readings have produced some interesting results. For example, Eleazar Fernandez's reading of the Exodus from a Filipino-American perspective departs from the traditional pattern of "conquest," "liberation," and "release," and situates the narrative within a rubric of immigration and settlement. Similarly, Uriah Kim has drawn attention to Uriah the Hittite, whose struggle for identity is akin to that of Asian Americans but often gets lost in the David-Bathsheba scandal.

Where do you see scholarship heading in this particular area? What do you see as the future agenda?

As to the future, finding solace in the familiar practices of the homeland should give way to acquiring a new identity and addressing the potential and problems of the new habitat. Diasporic readings tend to suffer from the burden of seeking simplistic parallels in the biblical narratives. Future diasporic reading must go beyond identifying with biblical characters and events. Going back to the biblical sources reinforces the notion that the Semitic tradition sets the norm for diasporic experiences. The biblical diasporic accounts do not address the New World Order and the international politics one faces today. There is also a "culture fetish" — an idealization of culture that overlooks and underplays some of the virulent and oppressive tendencies embedded in our cultures.

Most of the writing rightly celebrates the hyphenated identities of diaspora persons, and their discourse is laced with words such as "hybridity," "in-betweenness," "liminality," "Third Space," and so on. These hybridized identities, however, have been appropriated in a narrow sense to indicate the experiences of once-colonized and largely middle-class people who are trying to find an identity and selfhood in the Western metropolises. This ignores the vast amount of internal displacement that takes place within a country and the trauma these people go through. Sri Lanka and Darfur are examples of this.

Hybridity has become an over-used word, a soft option, and it is perceived as a one-size term fitting all conditions. It is simply seen as mixing or remixing certain distinct features of cultures without undergirding this with a serious political agenda. In these respects, diasporic writing is largely determined by the interests and agenda of the academy. Diasporic interpretation should move beyond idealizing culture and redefining hyphenated identities and should spend energy on religious fundamentalism, suicide bombings, and asylum-seeking, all of which have a great impact on our lives.

You are part of that group of scholars whose place of origin is outside the West but who for a variety of reasons find themselves functioning in the academic institutions of the West. What are some of the key issues or problems faced by this group?

The main concern has been well articulated by the African American playwright August Wilson. In one of his speeches, he said that when slaves were asked to perform before their white masters and their guests, they started a tradition of theater as amusement for the whites. This amusement was largely made up of whatever the slaves perceived or anticipated that their master wanted to see and hear. I have a fear that the diasporic and ethnic minority interpreters are falling into this trap and trying to tailor their material for white consumption. Ever since Edward Said, the question keeps coming up, are we simply reorientalizing the orient? The trick is how to make the texts speak as they spoke to those who produced them.

The other fear is of being co-opted by the mainstream. Look at what has happened to liberation theology. Once it came with the warning, "Do not try this at home, this is only for Third World countries." Now that it has been deftly woven into the concerns of the mainstream, the radical potency of liberation hermeneutics has been neutered. I remember the words of the American humorist Art Buchwald: "If you attack the establishment hard enough and long enough, they will make you a member of it."

In the "border crossing" context how do you see yourself? As an Asian or as a professionally qualified scholar? What is paramount to you — your Asianness or your status as a trained biblical interpreter?

This is one of the questions that keeps coming up — whether I am a biblical scholar who is an Asian or, for that matter, Sri Lankan, or an Asian who happens to be a biblical scholar. Some who are engaged in minority hermeneutics claim that they are basically biblical scholars and as such their work should be seen purely as biblical interpretation. This is music to the ears of liberals. If I say that I am a biblical scholar per se without any social-cultural context, then I fully fit in with the image of the mainstream, which expects scholars to have no cultural or ideological baggage. This, though, naturally annoys the Asians, who would see it as a forsaking of cultural roots. If, however, I say I am Asian, then the mainstream pigeonholes me and expects me to confine myself to dealing with ethnic matters. Asians, on the other hand, expect me to be their ambassador and not a *dhobi* washing our dirty hermeneutical linen in public. I think I would like to be both — Asian and a biblical scholar. I don't see the labels — professional or ethnic — as problematic. I think we can use this twin designation to our advantage. Since some of us have "made it," we can use this state of relative influence to place our concerns and issues in the mainstream discourse.

In the practice of cross-cultural hermeneutics, what has been your goal?

My goal is very simple. There is this great interest in minority hermeneutics and the interpretations that are emerging from our part of the world. The important thing is not to allow the mainstream to see these articulations as an exotic extra, or as an add-on to the previously determined Eurocentric curriculum. I have had experiences of giving a one-time lecture to a class on the Gospel of John in order to bring an Indian perspective, and to a Pauline theology class to say something about a liberation perspective. The important thing is to recognize and acknowledge these discourses as integral to the discipline called biblical studies. The aim is to radicalize the perception of the discipline and broaden its scope. What the former chairman of the BBC, Greg Dyke, said of the corporation — "It is hideously White" — could equally have been said of biblical studies. There are areas of biblical studies where our presence is virtually nil. No one among us is actively involved with the Dead Sea Scrolls, the Nag Hammadi Library, Gnostic studies, or biblical archeology. I would like to see Asian, African, Latin American, Caribbean, and Pacific scholars getting involved and bringing a set of different cultural, political, and hermeneutical questions to these areas of biblical studies. As a discipline, biblical studies is basically Eurocentric, and from its inception as a discipline it has served Western needs.

How do you incorporate your scholarship in cross-cultural hermeneutics into your teaching? How do your students, most of whom are raised in the West, receive this? What obstacles do you face?

This is a complicated issue that deserves a lengthy response, but let me explain it by giving an example. When I introduce *Dalit, Burakumin,* tribal, and feminist interpretations, students tend to treat them as interesting interpretations that are happening "over there." They also tend to

think that these have little importance for them except for the methodological issues these interpretations raise. To bring home the point that
these interpretations are not simply exotic but have significance for the
life of my English students, I adopt the contrapuntal approach. For instance, when studying the people's reading of the Bible, I use the biblical
interpretation undertaken by Solentiname peasants during Somoza's rule
as an example of the ordinary reader's appropriation of the Bible. I then
juxtapose this reading with the seventeenth-century use of the Bible by
the English radicals. If you look at their interpretations carefully, you
will notice that both the Nicaraguan peasants and the English dissenters
show an extraordinary interest in the miseries and agonies of the people
and draw on a similar set of texts to confront oppressive rule. This history of the use of the Bible by the English Diggers and Levellers rarely
comes up even in regular biblical classes because it is written out by
the mainstream for not being scholarly. This early example from English
history enables students to know that radical religious thinking is not
something that happens only overseas but is part of their history too. In
this way students reconnect with their history and get to analyze both
their own interpretative tradition and that of the Third World. Juxta-
posing these texts helps students to see mutual hermeneutical potentials
and perils.

*What will the landscape of biblical scholarship look like twenty
years from now?*

I can't imagine anything exciting happening. As a discipline, biblical
scholarship has an inherent disadvantage. The basic data we deal with —
the Bible — is old, fixed, and fragmentary, and it has been squeezed
for meaning from every conceivable angle — from supporting vegetar-
ianism to the veiling of women in church. Whereas other disciplines
come up with fresh data, we are stuck with palimpsests of the one
document. Occasionally, we come across new material such as the Nag
Hammadi Library or the Gospel of Judas. These discoveries do not on
the whole move the debate on except to produce in-house scholarly debates. Most of the time, what goes on in biblical studies is discussion
among biblical scholars. Although they claim that they are trying to recover and reconstruct the "original" meaning, what in actuality they are
engaged in is an endless and at times pointless discussion of each other's
scholarship. Most of the scholarly works in biblical studies, to use the

Gramscian phrase, is "elaboration upon elaboration." I find most of these discussions boring and petty.

As things stand today, biblical scholarship will become more and more fragmented among smaller and smaller interest groups. Look at the proliferation of groups, sections, and seminars at the annual meetings of the Society of Biblical Literature (SBL). At the last meeting in Washington (2006) I counted at least five different clusters of papers on Paul. The papers tackled topics that were so esoteric and narrow that they had interest only to die-hard Paul enthusiasts. The message is clear: "If you are not a hyper-specialist on Paul, don't bother." At the last annual meeting, I was there in a session (I must hasten to add that it was not on Paul) that had more presenters on the podium than in front of it. The scholarly work generated by the Research Assessment Exercise (RAE) in the United Kingdom will make the field even narrower and more specific. In an attempt to prove that they are research-active, academics in the UK are going to please their peers by churning out articles that will remain largely unread. The splitting of the Society of Biblical Literature from the American Academy of Religion (AAR) will have a disastrous effect on the SBL, but less so on the AAR. Mainstream scholarship will go on in these smaller, isolated communities as a way of bonding together as well as a way to share esoteric findings and to keep at bay unwanted external influences. What these conversations will produce are "yawns of familiarity."

The running of university departments is now becoming a preserve of academic managers rather than gentleman scholars, and the trend is toward courses on the Bible that will not substantially reference the Bible. The study of the Bible will not be undertaken in isolation but will be yoked to other attractive subject areas, such as film, literature, music, theater, and political journalism. Recently, I noticed one of the leading universities in the UK offering a course on the Hebrew Bible limited to three chapters: Nehemiah 4–6. Conjoining the Bible with these other disciplines will not only rescue it from such a sterile and narrow approach but will also provide new ways of asking questions and opening up new insights and potential. In such a diversified environment, the Bible should get both a new lease on life and a fresh look. As it becomes intellectually and financially untenable to maintain single-discipline courses, it is an interesting possibility that the Bible will find its home alongside other curricular subjects.

What I would like to see happen also is a vigorous debate between biblical scholars and Indologists and a revisiting of the question of hermeneutical connections between the Mediterranean world and India. The nineteenth-century Indologists identified some potential mutual influences between early Christianity and Buddhist thought. This has not been followed through due to political and ecclesiastical intervention. At a time when each and every religion is asserting it own uniqueness, the time is right for another look at this connection. It will not be easy. The biblical discipline as it stands is constrained by its methodological and theological presuppositions and so is prevented from undertaking such a task. Its application of the historical methods thrives on distinguishing different layers of texts, fetishising differences, and sanctifying a singular expression of sources.

More pertinently, biblical scholarship is largely a Christian or Jewish enterprise. Most of the practitioners involved in it are critical to a point but fundamentally sympathetic to the Christian or Jewish cause. Their interpretative approach is framed and driven by their religious allegiance and motivation. I don't see much hope of this dialogue between the Mediterranean world and India occurring because biblical studies remains a Eurocentric as well as Christian-centric discipline, and scholars won't do any thing that will weaken the twin pillars of Western civilization and Christianity — Hebraic and Hellenistic influences.

As far as the Third World and minority discourses are concerned, there is a stalemate now. The once vigorous *Dalit, minjung, Burakumin,* and Third World feminist hermeneutics seem to have run their course. Latin American liberation theology is now going back to its cultural roots and trying to recover liberative potential within its cultural resources — an enterprise that the Indians and Africans attempted from the nineteenth century on. Where cultures are being homogenized in the name of globalization, I think the future lies in negotiating between vernacular and cosmopolitan cultures. Such a "vernacular cosmopolitanism" will be a constant translation between indigenous and imported cultures, where no culture is fundamentally privileged over the other and each is called upon to question and rework both its pleasing and its despicable cultural practices in the light of the multidirectional exchange. Vernacular cosmopolitan hermeneutics is an enterprise that embeds native and international norms and values in such a way that they are present but transmuted. This mutual reinforcement of the local and international should yield rich hermeneutical dividends.

What are some of the exciting things happening in the theological or biblical fields outside of the West?

One exciting event was the formation of the Society of Asian Biblical Studies (SABS). There were nearly thirty biblical scholars from Asia at the inaugural meeting in Hong Kong last July. I am certain that, under the leadership of Archie Lee and Monica Melanchthon, it will grow and achieve great things. My hope is that the SABS will not replicate the sins of the dominant academic guilds.

Another exciting example is the new interest in the Bible as a classroom text in universities in China, India, Hong Kong, and the Philippines. This is a new departure. Generally the Bible is taught only in seminaries in Asia. Now it is being introduced as a cultural text to students who are not professed Christians. It will be interesting to see what sort of hermeneutics such teaching will produce. I hear that the Chinese church leadership, which has hitherto assumed a proprietorial role in interpreting the Bible, is finding it difficult to accept that the power of interpretation has been taken from them.

Thus far, which one of your writings do you consider as your favorite? For what reason? Currently, what are you working on?

What is my favorite writing? As Frank Wesley, the Indian painter said, "The next one." It is not the end-result but the process of writing that itself gives me satisfaction. I tremendously enjoy this. More specifically, rewriting. I make endless drafts. This is the only thing I can do. I can't even change an electric light bulb! When a manuscript is completed, I feel both exhausted and elated, but at the same time I also feel dispossessed and deprived because once the manuscript goes out of my hands it is no longer mine. I see each piece of writing as a response to a context or to contextual needs, and when a new context throws up new questions you move on to tackle them. Interpretation is essentially a process, not an achievement.

WORKS BY
R. S. SUGIRTHARAJAH

Books and Edited Volumes

Asian Faces of Jesus. Edited volume. Maryknoll, NY: Orbis Books, 1993.

Readings in Indian Christian Theology. Edited volume with Cecil Hargreaves. London: SPCK Press, 1993.

Frontiers in Asian Christian Theology: Emerging Trends. Edited volume. Maryknoll, NY: Orbis Books, 1994.

Asian Biblical Hermeneutics and Postcolonialism: Contesting the Interpretations. Maryknoll, NY: Orbis Books, 1998.

The Postcolonial Bible. Edited volume. Sheffield: Sheffield Academic Press, 1998.

Vernacular Hermeneutics. Edited volume. Sheffield: Sheffield Academic Press, 1999.

Dictionary of Third World Theologies. Edited volume with Virginia Fabella. Maryknoll, NY: Orbis Books, 2000.

The Bible and the Third World: Precolonial, Colonial and Postcolonial Encounters. Cambridge: Cambridge University Press, 2001.

Postcolonial Criticism and Biblical Interpretation. Oxford: Oxford University Press, 2002.

Postcolonial Reconfigurations: An Alternative Way of Reading the Bible and Doing Theology. St. Louis: Chalice Press, 2003.

The Bible and Empire. Postcolonial Explorations. Cambridge: Cambridge University Press, 2005.

The Postcolonial Biblical Reader. Edited volume. Malden, MA, and Oxford: Blackwell Publishing, 2005.

Wilderness: Essays in Honor of Frances Young. Edited volume. Journal for the Study of the New Testament Supplement Series. Edinburgh: T&T Clark, 2005.

Voices from the Margin: Interpreting the Bible in the Third World. Revised and expanded edition. Maryknoll, NY: Orbis Books, 2006.

Postcolonial Commentary on the New Testament Writings. Edited volume with Fernando Segovia. Edinburgh: T&T Clark, 2007.

Still at the Margins: Biblical Scholarship Fifteen Years after the Voices from the Margin. Edited volume. Edinburgh: T&T Clark, 2007.

Essays and Articles

"Indian Cowboy, Hindu Christ." *One World* 49 (1979): 18–19.

"Conversion: An Open Letter." *One World* 61 (1980): 16.

"A Professor of Pluralism." *One World* 76 (1982): 19–20.

"An Imaginary Lecture on the Varieties of Indian Theology." *One World* 100 (1984): 18–20.

"The Syro-Phoenician Woman." *Expository Times* 98 (1986): 13–15.

"Why Use Commentaries?" *One World* 114 (1986): 8–9.

"Jesus I Know, Paul I Know, but Who Is God? Christology and Multi-faith Hermeneutics." *Modern Churchman* 29 (1987): 28–31.

"Luke's Second Volume and the Gentiles." *Expository Times* 100 (1989): 178–81.

"For You Always Have the Poor with You." *Asian Journal of Theology* 4 (1990): 102–7.

"Inter-faith Hermeneutics: An Example and Some Implications." *Mission Studies* 7, no. 1 (1990): 9–20.

"Jesus Research and Third World Christologies." *Theology* 93 (1990): 387–91.

"Wisdom, Q, and a Proposal for a Christology." *Expository Times* 102 (1990): 42–46.

"What Do Men Say Remains of Me?" *Asian Journal of Theology* 5 (1991): 331–37.

"The Widow's Mites Revalued." *Expository Times* 103 (November 1991): 42–43.

"Creating a Just Future: The Politics of Peace and the Ethics of Creation in a Threatened World." *International Review of Mission* 81 (1992): 324–26.

"Men, Trees and Walking: A Conjectural Solution to Mark 8:24." *Expository Times* 103 (March 1992): 172–74.

"The Way of Jesus Christ: Christology in Messianic Dimensions." *International Review of Mission* 81 (1992): 324–26.

"Commitment, Context and Text: Examples of Asian Biblical Hermeneutics." *Biblical Interpretation* 2 (1994): 251–376.

"Introduction and Some Thoughts on Asian Biblical Hermeneutics." *Biblical Interpretation* 2 (1994): 251–63.

"Kosuke Koyama: A Model for Intercultural Theology." *International Review of Mission* 83 (1994): 639–40.

"Lady Meng: A Liberative Play Using Common Folklore." In *Frontiers in Asian Christian Theology: Emerging Trends,* ed. R. S. Sugirtharajah, 130–37. Maryknoll, NY: Orbis Books, 1994.

"From Orientalist to Post-colonial: Notes on Reading Practices." *Asian Journal of Theology* 10, no. 1 (1996): 20–27.

"Orientalism, Ethnonationalism and Transnationalism: Shifting Identities and Biblical Interpretation." In *Ethnicity and the Bible,* ed. Mark Brett, 419–29. Leiden: E. J. Brill, 1996.

"The Texts Are Always with You: Christians and Their Bibles." *Hindu-Christian Studies Bulletin* 9 (1996): 8–13.

"Textual Cleansing: A Move from the Colonial to Postcolonial Version." *Semeia* 76 (1996): 7–19.

"Biblical Studies in India: From Imperialistic Scholarship to Postcolonial Interpretation." In *Teaching the Bible: The Discourses and Politics of Biblical Pedagogy,* ed. Fernando Segovia and Mary Ann Tolbert, 283–96. Maryknoll, NY: Orbis Books, 1998.

"A Brief Memorandum on Postcolonialism and Biblical Studies." *Journal for the Study of the New Testament* 73 (1999): 3–5.

"Imperial Critical Commentaries: Christian Discourse and Commentarial Writings in Colonial India." *Journal for the Study of the New Testament* 73 (1999): 83–112.

"Postcolonialism and Indian Christian Theology." *Studies in World Christianity* 5, no. 2 (1999): 229–40.

"Critics, Tools and the Global Arena." In *Reading the Bible in the Global Village,* 49–60. Atlanta: Society of Biblical Literature, 2000.

"Marketing the Testaments: Canongate and Their Pocket-sized Bibles." *Biblical Interpretation* 10 (2002): 221–44.

"Postcolonial Theory and Biblical Studies." In *Fair Play: Diversity and Conflicts in Early Christianity,* ed. Ismo Dunderberg, Christopher Tuckett, and Kari Syreeni, 541–52. Leiden, Boston, and Cologne: E. J. Brill, 2002.

"The End of Biblical Studies?" In *Toward a New Heaven and a New Earth,* ed. Fernando Segovia and Elisabeth Schüssler Fiorenza, 133–40. Maryknoll, NY: Orbis Books, 2003.

CONTRIBUTORS

Dr. Charles Amjad-Ali is Martin Luther King, Jr., Professor of Justice and Christian Community and Director of the Islamic Studies Program at Luther Seminary, St. Paul, Minnesota. He is the author of *Islamophobia or Restorative Justice: Tearing the Veil of Ignorance* (2006), and *A Look towards the Mountain: A Report of the Two Consultations on the Role and Future of the National Council of Churches in Pakistan* (1993). He co-authored with Christine Amjad-Ali *But the Spirit Gives Life: Contextual Readings in the Scriptures* (1993) and *Passion for Change: Reflections on the Healing Miracles in St. Mark*, a CSC monograph (1989).

Dr. S. Wesley Ariarajah is Professor of Ecumenical Theology at Drew University School of Theology, Madison, New Jersey. He is author of *Not without My Neighbor: Issues in Interfaith Relations* (1999), *Did I Betray the Gospel? The Letters of Paul and the Place of Women* (1996), *Gospel and Culture: An Ongoing Discussion within the Ecumenical Movement* (1994), and *Hindus and Christians: A Century of Protestant Ecumenical Thought* (1991).

Dr. Musa W. Dube teaches in the Department of Theology and Religious Studies, the University of Botswana, Gaborone, Botswana. She is author of *The HIV&AIDS Bible: Some Selected* Essays (2007) and *Postcolonial Feminist Interpretations of the Bible* (2000). She has edited *HIV/AIDS and the Curriculum: Methods of Integrating HIV/AIDS in Theological Programs* (Geneva: WCC, 2003), and, with Musimbi Kanyoro, *Grant Me Justice: HIV/AIDS and Gender Readings of the Bible* (2004).

Dr. Kwok Pui-lan is the William F. Cole Professor of Christian Theology and Spirituality at the Episcopal Divinity School, Cambridge, Massachusetts. Her recent books include *Postcolonial Imagination and Feminist Theology* (2005), *Discovering the Bible in the Non-Biblical World* (1995), and the co-edited volumes, *Off the Menu: Asian and*

171

Asian North American Women's Religion and Theology (2007) and *Empire and the Christian Tradition: New Readings of Classical Theologians* (2007).

Dr. Archie C. C. Lee is Professor in the Department of Cultural and Religious Studies, the Chinese University of Hong Kong, Shatin, Hong Kong. He co-authored *Doing Theology with Asian Resources: Ten Years in the Formation of Living Theology in Asia* (1993). He is the Associate Editor of the *Global Bible Commentary* (2004). His many publications in Chinese include *Texts and Interpretations: Contemporary Meaning of the Old Testament* (1998) and *The Asian Context and Biblical Hermeneutics* (1996).

Dr. Monica Jyotsna Melanchthon is Professor of Old Testament Studies and Women's Studies at Gurukul Lutheran Theological College and Research Institute, Chennai, India. She is the author of *Rejection by God: The History and Significance of the Rejection Motif in the Hebrew Bible* (2001).

Dr. D. N. Premnath is Academic Dean and Associate Professor of Biblical Studies at St. Bernard's School of Theology and Ministry, Rochester, New York. He is the author of *Eighth Century Prophets: A Social Analysis* (2003).

Dr. Jean Pierre-Ruiz is Associate Professor at St. John's University, New York, Editor-in-Chief of the *Journal of Hispanic/Latino Theology* and Associate Editor of the *Catholic Biblical Quarterly.*

Dr. M. Thomas Thangaraj is the D. W. and Ruth Brooks Associate Professor of World Christianity at the Candler School of Theology, Emory University, Atlanta, Georgia. He is author of *The Common Task: A Theology of Christian Mission* (1999) and *The Crucified Guru: An Experiment in Cross-cultural Christology* (1994).

INDEX